Famahan SAMAKÉ

BINGUÉ, THE OTHER SIDE OF THE MEDAL

Novel
To all the black migrants in Bingué,
To the broken families,
And to the dreams in tatters.

BINGUÉ, THE OTHER SIDE OF THE MEDAL

This is a novel, any resemblance to real people or places is pure coincidence.

Copyright © 2023
All Rights Reserved

All rights reserved. No part of this publication may be reproduced, distributed, or transmitted in any form or by any means, including photocopying, recording, or other electronic or mechanical methods, without the prior written permission of the publisher, except in the case of brief quotations embodied in critical reviews and certain other non-commercial uses permitted by copyright law.

About the Author

Dr Famahan SAMAKÉ was born on March 19th 1970 in Kouban, in the old county of Odienné, in Côte d'Ivoire. He holds a PhD in French Literature of the XIXth Century and he specialises in Émile Zola and naturalism. He is a dual British and Ivorian citizen who currently works as a lecturer at the Alassane Ouattara University in Bouaké, in Côte d'Ivoire. He is also a columnist, an essayist, a novelist, a playwright, a literary critic, a translator and a corrector for both general and Christian literature.

Table of Contents

PART ONE ....

    Chapter 1 2

    Chapter 2 20

    Chapter 3 32

    Chapter 4 43

PART TWO ....

    Chapter 1 56

    Chapter 2 69

    Chapter 3 81

    Chapter 4 93

PART THREE ....

    Chapter 1 107

    Chapter 2 119

    Chapter 3 131

    Chapter 4 140

PART FOUR ....

    Chapter 1 153

    Chapter 2 164

    Chapter 3 176

PART FIVE ....
   Chapter 1 189
   Chapter 2 199
   Chapter 3 209
   Chapter 4 218

PART ONE

WHEN THE WORLD COLLAPSES AROUND ME

Chapter 1

When the reservoir of tears dries up to the point
where you can no longer cry out

On this afternoon of June 7th 2017, I was arrested by the Morthuria Police, which covers the metropoles of Neuchastel and of Portalier, in the Bottecôte county, in the North-East of this country of Bingué. Since then I am lost in my thoughts in this small cell at the central Police station of Neuchastel. They call it a cell but for me, it is a prison, no less. A four square meter cell, with a small elevation of concrete of about ten centimetres high on which a single mattress covered with a navy blue plastic is laid out. There are no bed sheets here at my disposal and the mattress is as hard as a rock. Then on the left-hand side, the toilet, and a sink where I can wash my face and brush my teeth. The metallic door is so heavy that it can easily weigh a quarter of a ton. Nothing can be seen through it, although there is a small window in the middle of it that can only be opened from the outside, when the Police wants to talk to me, the detainee. It then slams shut again to send me back to my isolation, and to my long-lost freedom. What the hell did I do to end up in this prison ?

However, everything had started very well that morning. Earlier in the day, I felt very comfortable because I had had a great night. It was half past six when I woke up. I washed my face very quickly before awaking my two little girls aged nine and eight, Alesha and Lydia. They had a bath and got dressed up before I took them to school. This is the daily routine of a single father living with young children, or rather the routine of any single parent here in Bingué.

In the meantime, I prepared their breakfast. On the menu, omelettes, toast with mayonnaise for Lydia and margarine for Alesha, with coffee with milk for each one of them.

Later that afternoon, I made them French fries and alloco, fried plantains that we love so much in our native Ebrounia, and oven roasted chicken thighs. Alesha only eats chicken thighs; she wouldn't eat the wings or any other part of the chicken. The meal is ready and I'm just waiting for the girls to make their way to the dining table. Rather, I am expecting them to come home and sit down to eat with their big brother, Joshua, who had come back from his university to spend a few days with us in Portalier. As for me, I am on my second day of fasting out of the three days that I have been dedicating to the Lord for the past four months. So, I won't eat anything before six o'clock this evening.

Joshua gave me a hand. He would pick up his young sisters from St. Paul's Anglican School in Portalier, just five hundred meters from the family home while I put the finishing touches to my culinary recipe for the day.

He quickly returned home with a sibylline word from the Headteacher of the children's school: *"Your children are not here. You know where they are.'*

I was taken aback by that word from the Headteacher, which meant nothing to me. I then decided to go and ask for an explanation. So, I went up to my room to put on some pants and a shirt when, suddenly, Joshua knocked on my door:

- The police downstairs are here to talk to you, he said.

I went downstairs and met them. The boy hadn't told me there were so many of them: three men and two women, in police uniforms, with two police cars parked in my backyard. I greeted them and one of them, probably the head of the delegation, very tall and wearing a navy blue jacket, asked me the following question, to make sure he had identified me correctly:

- ''Doctor Bamba?'', asked a Police officer.
- ''Yes, it's me'', I answered.
- ''Do you know Alesha Bamba and Lydia Bamba?'', he asked.
- ''Of course, they are my daughters. What is going on with them?'', I asked him.
- '' You are under arrest for assault, battery, negligence, child cruelty, etc. You don't have to say anything; but anything you say may be held against you in a court of law. Did you understand?'', he said.
- ''What is it, officer? What am I being blamed for?'', I asked the Police officer.
- ''We can't talk about it here. You need to come with us to the police station for questioning'', he replied.

- ''Well, let's go then. I am at your disposal'', I said, confidently.
- ''But we have to handcuff you first'', he replied.
- ''I can't see a reason why that is necessary. I oppose no resistance to you whatsoever and I am not dangerous as you can see. I prefer not to be handcuffed'', I said candidly.
- ''We have to put handcuffs on your wrists, it is the procedure for any arrest, whether the suspect is dangerous or not. We do this for your own protection'', he replied stoically.

After much hesitation, especially since my nineteen-year-old son was an eyewitness to the whole sorry scene worthy of Franz Kafka's **The Trial**, I was forced to accept they handcuff me. I was only given the choice between having my hands cuffed behind my back, or my hands cuffed in front of me. I decided that hands in my back with handcuffs were even more humiliating than my hands cuffed in the front. So, they chained me up while being kind enough to ask me if it was not too tight. Apparently, they wanted me to be comfortable in my chains!

I was then taken out of my home through the back door of the semi-detached house where I lived. The two female Police officers escorted me by flanking me right and left. I saw that the three men stayed behind and I complained about that. The female officers explained to me that they were going to search my home which was potentially a crime scene. I tried to oppose it, in vain, because after all, they did not present me any search warrant nor an arrest warrant either. I was then told that in this country of Bingué a search warrant is hardly necessary once a potential crime has been brought to the Police's attention. It could proceed to the arrest of the suspect without any other form of trial, or any need to request an arrest warrant, even less of a search warrant. In the end, I could only to sit in the back seat of this little police car, with one of the ladies sitting next to me, to keep an eye on me and put my seat belt on. After all, I no longer had any hands to carry out such a simple task myself.

In five minutes, we arrived at the central police station of the city, on the other bank of the river which gives its name to the region, the Thelmor. I was registered in their computer system as required: my name, address, and other personal information were entered into their database. They demanded that I take off my own clothes and put on those that the police had. They put me in an outfit worthy of a clown, clothes that were too loose, including jogging pants that were too jumpy and too large. On top of all that, they had no lace at the waist whatsoever! Apparently, there is always a fear that a detainee might commit suicide. But why would I ever consider committing suicide in the first place since I blamed myself for absolutely nothing? Besides, so far, I had absolutely no idea why I was arrested or why I was taken to the Police station I the first place for questioning.

Here was I all dressed up like a clown. They locked me up in this tiny cell. For the first time in my life, I was deprived of freedom. This baptism of fire in the prison environment sounded heavy to me. I thought, before this experience, that only real criminals experienced such infamy. A man like me, who thought he was so smart, educated, honest; a man who never had a single drop of alcohol in his entire life, nor tried any form of drug; a man who did not even smoke a cigarette, who never stole anything nor got into a fight; a man who never visits a bar or a nightclub; a man who hadn't even gone to the cinema for at least seven years, what could prepare him for a stay in prison?

But here I was! Locked up in a cell. Here I was in a mess. Here I was locked up between four walls, on a simple denunciation from my nine-year-old daughter, Alesha, a student in year five. That child, emerging from my urine, would she become the crocodile that would swallow me? I now understand the meaning of this Diula proverb, the African tribe to which I belong.

I am lost in my thoughts. Today, I try to imagine what Alesha told her teachers about me to prompt them to alert the social services and the Police which eventually put me under arrest. I am digging into my memories to see where and when I have offended her. What have I done to her for her to tell them that I beat her up? But what surprises me most is the apparent long list of reasons for the arrest: *child cruelty, assault, battery, neglect, etc*. What does this et cetera mean anyway? What fiction could she have told them so that they came against me with a large team of five policemen driven in two cop vehicles?

Already an hour and a half that I am locked in this cell, an hour and a half spent without seeing the light of day, nor the outside for that matter. It was half past three when I was put in handcuffs in my living room. Now it's five o'clock. A policeman comes to pick me up and take me to an interrogation room. A man and a lady soon join me there. They sit in front of me, with an analogue tape recorder, to record the interview. Here we like to do it the old-fashioned way. They read me my rights before starting.

The male policeman speaks first and gives me the details of Alesha's accusations against me. My daughter allegedly claimed that I frequently hit her with my belt and kicked her in the stomach while I was wearing my shoes. She also claimed to have several scars and bruises on her body to prove it. She went on to claim that she is a beaten and an abused child. Also, apparently, I left them alone at home, her little sister Lydia and herself to go to town, even at night. She also claimed that I starved them by banning them form eating food for several days in a row in order to punish them. That afternoon, as the interrogation was being carried out, the two girls were being examined by three consultant paediatricians at the university hospital of Neuchastel. Clearly, the police wanted them to be examined thoroughly by experts in order to get to the bottom of this whole affair.

I was stunned and I fell down from the clouds. If I don't hear that coming from Alesha, personally, I cannot believe that that little girl - who hasn't even turned ten yet -- could have said such nonsense about me. By the way, she would turn exactly ten in just a week.

The Police then asked me specific questions about Alesha's charges. I get asked about what she called the last time I hit her. It was, according to her accusations, in Bardamia, at the Notans', friends of mine whom we had visited during the half-term school holiday, from May 28th to June 4th, 2017. I am supposed to have hit her on Wednesday, May 31st. I am delighted to hear that she was able to say something very specific like that because then we would have witnesses, the likes of Muriel and Adnan Notan, and potentially, their daughter Malia, should have surely witnessed that battery. The charges of food deprivation have no merit either. I explained to the two police officers that the same day, I had just roasted chicken thighs in the oven and made French fries and fried plantains for their lunch, not to mention that, like every day, they ate in their school canteen. Every week, I paid the €20 for their school meals in the canteen although they are entitled to free meals since I had been out of work from mid-December 2016. I was getting unemployment benefits which allowed me to claim free school meals for my children. I refused to let them eat at school for free as disadvantaged students, or the so-called pupil premium. It is a fancy designation to refer to the children of destitute parents. I stubbornly refused to let anybody use the terms of pupil premium when referring to any my children because as a teacher myself, I knew absolutely everything about the stigma attached to students branded as children of the poor in schools throughout this country of Bingué. They are ostracised, minimised and encouraged to aim very low in life, as if the children of the poor were incapable of being intelligent and of aspiring to the highest positions in society.

Anyway, during my interrogation, I argued that since three police officers stayed behind at my house to search it, they could not have failed to see the chocolate and vanilla ice creams that are in the freezer, let alone the bag of rice, the bags of potatoes, the bags of French fries in the freezer and all the condiments that are in the kitchen, as well as the fresh fish, the meat and the uncooked chicken legs that are in the fridge, not to mention all that I had cooked for them for the three-thirty meal. I pointed out that they had breakfast that morning before going to school, like every day, and that at night they eat a light meal before going to bed. That's at least four daily meals, including the school dinner that I pay out of my pocket despite my being unemployed for the past six-months. I was making that sacrifice to protect them against the stigma of children who get free school meals.

I asked them why I had not been told anything about the accusations made by Lydia so far. They answered me nothing on that matter but they solely focused rather on what Alesha had brought against me. I also asked them what the consultant paediatricians who examined them at the Neuchastel University Hospital did say about all those serious allegations. Again, I got no answers.

Overall, I denied all of Alesha's charges, including the charge of negligence. I was told, however, that I used to go out at night and leave my young daughters home alone. I was surprised by such a ludicrous accusation because I had no friends in the city and my only person I could call a friend in that metropole lived with us at home. I did not visit anyone; I did not go to the cinema; I had not been to a nightclub for at least the past twelve years. I did not go to any bar or pub since I don't drink nor smoke cigarette. I did not have a girlfriend and I had not chatted any woman up for years. I did not see any prostitutes nor did I ever turn up at any massage parlours. So, if I left my children alone at home at night to go out, where would I go? To do what?

After the questioning, I was taken back to my cell. I was once again confined to solitude. I could then think about everything Alesha blamed me for. It was simply staggering, to say the least.

What have I done to deserve such a sad fate? As a Malinké saying goes, the West African tribe which I come from, the crocodile that came out of my pee had just bitten me where it hurts the most. This nine-year-old girl had just taken my freedom away from me. Up until that point in time, I always thought this sort of things only happened to others, to hardened criminals who refused to change their ways. But now I had to let myself be put in handcuffs and driven to the police station! I suddenly realised that this could also happen to citizens who claim to be honest and to those who thought they were leading uneventful lives all along?

Then a few events rushed back to the surface of my memory like the handwritten notes of my daughter Alesha where she wrote that she was in danger and that she needed help. I specifically remember one such letter that I discovered in her room while I was cleaning it up around Christmas 2016, a note addressed to LignEnfant in which she cried out for help, alleging that she was badly beaten up by her father and that she wanted the authorities to intervene to free her from his punitive hands. I remember that with Claudia, we had interrogated her to find out where this so-called mistreatment that she was denouncing in her letter had occurred. She had been asked when she had been physically abused by me, and on what part of her body had been struck by my blows?

In response, she simply claimed that it had never happened in Portalier but that it had happened in Bardamia when she was six years old. I then remembered this sentence from Claudia:

- So, my daughter Alesha, you don't ever forgive nor forget? You won't ever forgive even your dad if he hit you almost four years ago? You continue to ruminate a fierce anger against him all those years, and you are determined to destroy his whole life, his career, to quench your thirst for revenge?

Well, coming back to what matters today, it was around 7 p.m. when I was freed from my tiny cell and asked to go home without charge. However, I was told that the procedure will follow its course and that if the investigation required it, I would be called upon to attend the police station as a free witness. The objects that were found on me when I was admitted to my cell were returned to me, including my clothes. I changed my outfit worthy of a clown and wore my own clothes and took immediately the road that leads to my house. It was some two or three kilometres further down south.

I cannot tell whether I was consumed by anger, rage or bitterness. As someone that always thought such things only happened to others! There was I, in the middle of a legal whirlwind without having any idea about how to handle the problem, nor how to solve it very quickly once and for all. I was walking without realising how my legs carried me from the Neuchastel courthouse to my home some two or three kilometres further down south. Mechanically, however, I advanced, putting one foot in front of the other, one step at a time, to see if I could complete my nonchalant journey at all. I was in no hurry to go home because no young children were waiting for me there. Besides, I wanted to think, to try to analyse my situation, to understand my ordeal, if that were ever possible.

Still, I found myself at home at some point. I do remember it was around 8 p.m. by then when I returned to this semi-detached house which was once a so beautiful and a so joyful place to live in in my eyes but which looked so desperately empty at that precise hour in time. It was true that my daughters were no longer there. I did not know where Alesha and Lydia would spend the night nor did I know where they would spend the following night. What did it matter anyway? They wanted to get away from me; they would therefore bear the consequences of their actions.

I found Joshua well at home and although we said so little to each other, he understood that I had been released on bail, pending further investigation. I only asked him what the three male policemen did in my house, whether they entered my bedroom or not. He replied that yes they did and that they took away some documents of mine. I therefore sought to circumscribe their actions. I realised that they had searched my briefcase which was exposed in the middle of the bed. That was so easy for them, I told myself.

I searched it in my turn and quickly realised that I had lost our flight tickets that I bought thanks to a loan from Fadel Khanam who lived in Washington at the time. Valid and expired passports were also taken away, along with birth certificates and other such documents. My belts were taken away, presumably to support Alesha's outlandish and outrageous accusations that I whipped her with my black belt just five days before. The bedroom wasn't as messy as I expected, though.

I therefore understood that my trip with my daughters to Ebrounia which was scheduled for July 21th was very compromised indeed, to say the least. If I could collect the flight tickets online, I could not easily collect the passports. Even the expired passports of my other children had been taken away, my children born to my estranged wife and who lived much further down south, in Luthor, those expired passports were all taken away from my house without my knowledge nor consent. What was such an initiative all about?

Claudia had not come home from work just yet and she was completely unaware of the high drama that unfolded that afternoon. I was therefore impatiently awaiting her return to tell her about my misadventure with the children and the Police.

When she returned home that evening shortly after eight o'clock, I calmly told her of the drama that had taken place earlier in the day under our roof. She could not believe her ears. She was dumbfounded by it all and was so much more dejected and shocked by this turn of events than I was. There is no doubt, however, that this sort of reaction is inherent to ladies for they are prone to panicking over little things. Still, this time around, it was really tough. It seemed to me that she was even more frustrated to hear that the Police did put me in handcuffs before leaving my house, in broad daylight, like a vulgar common criminal, in front of my elder son. How could a professional, a doctor and a professor of my kind be treated like this on one simple denunciation by a little megalomaniac and a narcissistic girl? How could one give more credit to the words of a little manipulator like Alesha than to those of a confirmed professional like me? And what was that mighty humiliation that I had been subjected to in front of my student son? All that because Alesha had made false claims to one of her classmates who lives in our neighbourhood? Claudia got lost in rhetorical questions that none of us could answer. And why did the white mother of that little girl not make the effort to come and ask me any questions, if only she wanted to verify the authenticity of the information that her daughter provided her with? On what basis did she rush to the Headteacher of the primary school that our children attended together to tell her such low-level gossip?

Little by little, we realised the obvious: the dream she had had and in which Alesha soaked my diplomas and degrees was really a premonitory one that warned me against the upcoming misfortune that would threaten my career as a teacher here in Bingué. In that dream, Alesha was indeed holding a canister of some sanitary product for toilets with a spout and she was spraying water on my degrees all over. This canister was filled with water and my daughter had her finger on the low crank of it, as if she was holding the trigger of a gun. She sprinkled my eight diplomas spread out in front of her in two rows of four diplomas each. The CEPE, BEPC, Baccalauréat A2 and CAP/CEG diplomas were aligned on the lower line while the upper line contained the bachelor degree, master's degree, DEA and PhD. Alesha had her finger on the trigger and was ostensibly wetting my degrees by pouring as much water on them as needed, with a smirk of satisfaction and bliss on her face. Sometimes, she would go back and pour further water on the pieces of paper that were not wet enough for her liking.

Assessing today's events, we were in agreement that we were then in complete fulfilment of that premonitory dream. It was obvious that this affair could potentially make all my diplomas and degrees obsolete, forcing me to work like the millions of migrants without qualifications, those who resign themselves to becoming warehouse operatives or factory workers that continue to operate in Bingué in a context of excessive relocation. Especially the second dream she had in April was ever so accurate. In it, Alesha was telling a lot of nonsense about me, surrounded by three white ladies who seemed to be taking a lot of notes since Alesha was speaking with great self-confidence and eloquence that seemed far beyond her young age. The notes taken by those ladies went on for pages and pages, but my nine-year-old daughter continued to charge me relentlessly with a barrage of accusations. We agree that both dreams were translated into contingent reality on that fateful day.

A long time ago, I had established the link between my dreams - or the dreams referring to me – with true future events in my life. I had come to the conclusion that they announced beforehand the mains events to come, be it luck or misfortune. The examples were legion and I could not name them all. For example, sometimes I had seen in a dream that I was sitting exams a few days before those examinations were submitted to us. And, strangely enough, I discovered that the questions that I had answered in my dream were exactly the same questions that I had to deal with in reality. So, I always felt like the exam paper was a déjà vu. Often times, before losing a job or finding a new one, I lived exactly those phenomena in my dreams. Sometimes, I would have the dream three days prior to things happening in the physical exactly the same way as they did in the spiritual realm. I had also defended my PhD in my dreams at least five days before the d-day and the comments made by my examiners in the spiritual realm were exactly those they put to me on the day in the physical. Rarely, I was surprised at the main events that unfolded in my life. Somehow I was always prepared in advance.

I clearly considered that my friend Claudia's dreams had prepared me for what I was going through on June 7, 2017 in Neuchastel. I felt that the wine was already drawn and that we would have to drink it. However, after my friend Claudia's first dream, in December 2016, I understood that this child would do me enormous harm by making some ludicrous and unsubstantiated claims against me. I had planned to send her back to Ebrounia with her mother, Maryline, so that she could continue her studies in Babiville. Besides, I could then concentrate on my work because the full-time care of the two children prevented me from working at all. I could no longer teach because I had to drop them off to school in the morning and pick them up immediately after school. Clearly I could not do it and carry out my work at the same time simply because I could have been in my classes anywhere in Hamford, in Wasberline, in Sunguin or in other small towns around Neuchastel when I was supposed to drop them off to school or pick them up at the end of the school day.

That was the reason why I bought myself a plane ticket for the end of December 2016 to bring Alesha back to her mother in Africa. It was a pity I could not get her an emergency Ebrounian visa then. I had to wait for a more favourable moment to do so. It took me an awful lot of time to get her that visa and that turned out so badly for me!

Chapter 2

The kafkaian trials do not only happen in literature

The next day, Friday, June 8th, 2017, I was summoned to the Neuchastel courthouse for a hastily arranged hearing. It was my third and final day of fasting for that week and I was heading to court early, well before one-thirty. I was all dressed up in a grey suit and some litigants took me for a lawyer who had come to the rescue of some defendant! It made me smile despite the gloomy atmosphere of the Kafkaesque situation in which I was embedded.

Shortly afterwards, we were invited into the courtroom and that was when I was handed a whole blue binder filled with pages of various accusations all levied against me by Alesha alone. There were no less than forty pages of literature to read and I could not digest them all right away, especially since I was accused of all those crimes detailed on no less than thirteen pages in all. The rest were procedural matters and brief reports from the consultant paediatricians who examined the two girls the day before.

I note with relief that they have concluded, unanimously, that none of the girls bore the slightest trace of physical violence that could be associated with domestic abuse. However, they recommended, that given the seriousness of the allegations against me and all the details given by Alesha, it would be appropriate to take precautionary measures to protect the little girls from any hint or threat of violence.

I was also vindicated in my first opinion that none of those allegations came from Lydia. Indeed, it was mentioned there that she denied all the charges Alesha made against me, insisting that everything was fine at home and that Alesha was lying to the authorities. I even learnt that she was crying under the scrutiny of the many questions that were put to her, hoping that she would corroborate her sister's claims.

However, I was flabbergasted by the insinuations of the social worker who concluded that Lydia was obviously too thin and did not seem to reach the normal weight of an eight-year-old child, which, in her humble opinion, demonstrated that the girls were not sufficiently nourished as Alesha asserted. If therefore Lydia denied everything outright, there was no doubt in the social worker's mind that she was afraid of any reprisals from her violent parent, she suggested without a shred of evidence. I was dumbfounded by such nonsense - and innuendo - which had no tangible basis whatsoever. I asked myself: so, what is the ideal, or minimum, weight of an eight-year-old child in Bingué? What was the law that established or determined such weight? Did the social worker bring a scale with her the day before - on June 7th, 2017 - to St. Paul School in Portalier to weigh my children before concluding that' *''obviously Lydia did not reach the normal weight of an eight years old child''*? Even when children of the same age are fed exactly the same meals, and in exactly the same quantity and at the same times, do they grow at the same rate and weigh the same weight? Do all eight-year olds necessarily have the same weight? Are those who are thin necessarily malnourished while those who are overweight are better nourished? If bad faith could kill!

But the gold medal for the biggest liar goes to my daughter Alesha who lined up a lengthy litany of very serious allegations against me. She did not even shy away from giving dates of extreme physical attacks in front of witnesses! She thus stated that the last time she was hit her violently dated back to the previous Sunday, June 4th, 2017, at our home at 73, Traiteur Cour, in Portalier. She told the police that I had beaten her up badly that day, in my room because I found a letter she had written to denounce the abuse she suffered at my hand. I would have whipped her with my belt before kicking her in the stomach with my shoes on my feet! She even specified that her grandmother, Claudia, had attended the outrageous scene. The latter was supposed to have asked me to stop beating her up so violently, which I was obviously supposed to have refused to do. I was simply in awe, frankly!

That denunciation contained three big lies: firstly, I summoned her to my room that evening on our return from Bardamia in the south-east of Bingué to scold her about a love letter that she had written for a boy in her class, a certain Joel. The content was too graphic to my liking and I let her know how I felt about that. Secondly, there was no beating nor hitting involved, not a single slap nor a blow from the belt, let alone any kicks in the abdomen whatsoever! Her older brother, Joshua, had come home from his University and was in the kitchen with Lydia at the time. Claudia was out of the house altogether at that exact moment in time. I was alone in my room when I remonstrated with Alesha. When we were done, looking very upset, she went down the stairs to join her siblings. I had no idea then that this was the last straw that was going to make Alesha's vase overflow and trigger the Police investigation the next couple of days.

Further along, on one of the many accusation pages, she claims that I also beat her on June 3rd, 2017 at the Notans' in Bardamia. I am told I have kicked her hard in the stomach that day while having my shoes on. If that were true, with my eighty kilograms, she should be bleeding internally! She even cited Muriel Notan and Adnan Notan, my friends, as having witnessed that barbaric act of extreme violence. I told myself that this was timely and handy since the investigation should be easy and quick since it cited a specific crime scene, a specific and recent date and even eyewitnesses who were all alive and available for questioning.

In short, the judge in charge of the case at the first hearing, a lady with shoulder-length black hair, gave me forty-five minutes to read the indictment before the hearing took place. I took the opportunity to read everything and the hearing started soon after.

Right away, I was told that there was absolutely no chance of getting my daughters back that day. The Council of Portalier was now positioning itself as the mother of my daughters and, in their interest, it proposed that the court snatched my children from me for a transitional period of six months, the time to elucidate the case a little better. It was all about procedural issues. They did not even want to talk about the merits of the case. No one tried to find out whether Alesha was telling the truth or not. What interested those people was to find out whether I was the biological father of the girls and whether or not I had parental authority over them. I was told that their school claimed that I had not provided any proof showing that I exercised parental authority over my daughters, especially since we were in a country where, traditionally, it was the mothers who exercised it.

I was asked for the identity of the mothers of my daughters and their telephone and electronic contacts. I stoically provided them with any such information. They mentioned the plane tickets that were found at my house during the search. I hastened to tell them that I had to go with the girls to Babiville, in Ebrounia, for the summer holidays so that they could spend time with their respective mothers. I was told that there was virtually no chance that I would be allowed to travel with them outside the country where binguist justice has no jurisdiction. I was still advised to make such a request at the next hearing scheduled for July 4th, 2017. Our flight tickets were valid from July 21st and the schedule seemed very tight to me. I might as well give up on that trip and brace myself to lose the €1200 that Fadel had lent me from Washington! How crazy was it to borrow money for three flight tickets that would be of absolutely no use? And still I would have to pay the money back in full in a short space of times.

When I tried to mention the lies contained in Alesha's accusations, no one wanted to hear about them. I was told this was just a procedural hearing. Finally, the judge decided that given the great details and the seriousness of the charges levied against me, for the safety of the girls, it was better to separate them from me for a while. That was designed to rule out any remote possibility of reprisals if they were given back to me immediately. We closed the hearing on that note and I went home with an empty head, with ideas flying around in all directions, like free electrons do, a bit like in a 3D film in which the bubbles fly and come towards you to the point where you think you can catch them with your hands.

On July 4th, therefore, I went to court a second time to try to clear my reputation. I hoped then that they would at least look at the merits of the case that time around. First constant: another judge was now in charge of the case. He was a tall and an elegant man, working on a MacBook Pro, wearing a sleek, well-tailored grey suit. It could be legitimately argued that he really had the look and prestige of a judge!

I noticed very quickly that we were still lost in technical details such as the desire of the Council of Portalier's lawyers to establish the identity of the mothers of my daughters by means of DNA tests. They also wanted to make sure that I was indeed the biological father of my daughters kidnapped by the municipal authorities. As I had prepared myself well with all the supporting documents, I produced the birth certificates of my children, which the judge brushed aside, arguing that anyone can have a birth certificate issued at their request and pass off other people's children as their own. I immediately understood that the judge did not mean that that was possible in Bingué. In his head, I assumed he meant that this possible in Africa. I confronted him with the legally binding DNA test that I had done to prove Lydia's parentage before she got her binguist passport. I told him that it is the DDC - Dna Diagnostic Center of Londamou - which carried it out. I also argued that it was indeed about the very first laboratory chosen by the binguist ministry of the Interior to carry out that kind of tests for cases of immigration by descent. Its results should, by no means, be therefore doubted. This DNA test was indeed initiated on the premises of the Bingué embassy in Darusha in the neighbouring country, Sénisso, and my sample was taken on the premises of the passport office of Gare Victrine de Londamou. However, without a logical explanation, the judge rejected it out of hand and even refuses to take the document. Instead, he demanded that we do a large DNA test that would include my daughters and I in addition to their respective mothers. He then chose a house connected to the University of Neuchastel to perform it. This test should determine if I was indeed the biological father of my two girls. It was also aimed at proving beyond doubt that the mothers assigned to them were indeed their biological mothers. Finally, it would determine if they were related to each other as half-sisters. In simple terms, all that scientific scenario was directed at verifying whether I was telling the truth since the beginning. They did not trust a single word I told them. They thought I was not even the biological father of my children. They assumed I did not disclose the true identity of their respective mothers either. Why would I ever lie on simple matters like these?

I made it very clear to the judge that I had already done a DNA test for at least Lydia and that I would not undergo any further DNA testing to prove to anyone that those girls were mine indeed since they were not picked up in the street. They were not wandering in some open fields nor in the bush at the time but at my house, bearing my name. I did bring them to this country of Bingué as my children although they were born in Africa. To do this, I already had to meet certain legal criteria to satisfy the Immigration services. I therefore refused to go back and travel the same way again. The judge told me that if I ever refused to submit myself to those new DNA tests, he would assume that I was not the biological father of any of my children in question. He added that he would also consider that I had something to hide. I was out of myself for I was consumed with anger. I always considered myself to be truthful and honest. I had told no lies in the life and would not begin a career as a liar in court! I told him that I did not care what he would think and that he could take whatever measures he wanted as I was done with that whole trial altogether.

I was scandalised by such absurd tactic of delay which was aimed at nothing other than stalling the process. For someone who was hoping to finally get to the bottom of the matter that day, and eventually, to be going home with his daughters like I was, it was simply too much to take in. I mentioned the fact that I had to travel with my daughters to Africa, in our native country from July 21th. I stressed that they would spend time with their respective mothers as I planned for quite a long time prior to the court case. The judge countered that since I refused to submit to his grand ensemble DNA test, why should he allow me to go on my long-planned family holiday with my daughters? He admittedly recognised that that trip was not prompted by that ongoing affair since I took my tickets at the beginning of last April, when there was no trouble on the horizon, but he still refused to allow me to go ahead with the trip. The main reason was, however, that I would leave his jurisdiction altogether. That was not going to happen, was it?

It was a real dialogue of the deaf that took place between us because their priorities were not mine and my priorities were very far from theirs. They acted like they had all the time in the world in front of them and I thought time was running out fast for me. I would like to move very quickly so that Alesha's allegations were refuted as quickly as possible and that I was allowed to return home with my daughters. However, the interests of justice seemed to be elsewhere, meaning poles apart from mine. Delaying the procedure and making it as elastic as possible seemed to be its main concern. That undoubtedly would allow the lawyers to put food on the table much longer because they would be able to hand in invoices showing that they worked several hours on that court case. They could claim they were trying to save two little black girls of African origin from the lacerated claws of their evil father as cruel as some real ogre from the Stone Age era! The judge would also be able to justify that he had carefully considered the whole question and its avenues over several months in a row before making a particular judgment in the best interests of the children.

I understood that that case was off to a very bad start indeed and that for at least six months, if not more, we would be dancing around some invisible ghosts. I told the judge that I felt like I was convicted before the end of the proceedings. I felt they were treating me as if I were guilty of serious abuse on my children until proved innocent. And I spelt it out when I said that I was standing before him as guilty until my innocence was proven. On hearing that, the judge got angry and told me, in an angry tone, that I was not guilty of anything so far and that no one in his court treated me as such. For him, I was not even tried yet and no one had found me guilty of anything.

I therefore decided to withdraw from the trial once and for all because I refused to participate in this travesty of justice for one more second since they refused to talk about the merits of the case all that time. In my perspective, we were just wasting a precious time I did not have.

Anyway, the judge suggested that if I made such a radical decision, at the conclusion of the procedure, he would make a judgment which would be against me for having chosen to desert the trial. I told him that I would assume the consequences of any decision that he would make from that point on. He adjourned the case on that note. When the lawyer for the Council of Portalier asked me a question afterwards, about some document that I had to make available to her as the proceedings required, I ask her:

- ''What trial are you talking about? Because I do not know of the existence of any lawsuit concerning me or my children!''. On that word, I walked away.

On hearing that, she understood that I was really carrying out my threat to withdraw from the procedure as of that day. The next court hearing was scheduled for August and I do not even remember the exact date because I simply could no more care less. That is how I lost my children, Alesha and Lydia. I did not see them again until the publication of this book. I only learned that for the first six months of their placement in foster care, the first white family that volunteered to take them in dropped out after those initial six months. That family had throwing in the towel because they found Alesha to be a very difficult child to handle. On the other hand, they had not experienced any problems with Lydia. But, as the two girls could not be separated, they washed their hands of them both.

Soon after that, another white family was to welcome them in their midst still in the region of Bottecôte. After three months, that other family got rid of the girls because of the actions of the indescribable Alesha. In less than twelve months, they had lived with four different families, including me, their father. God only knows where they are today.

Chapter 3

Let's throw the teacher out of his classroom, and fast !

When I returned home on July 4th, 2017, I felt alone: Joshua had left for Bardamia for a while already and Claudia chose to leave Neuchastel for good. She returned to Luthor while waiting to start a new life in France. So, I decide to go back to Bardamia where I taught the previous decade. At least there, I could go back to school and resume my career as a teacher. I had missed work a lot over the past six months, especially because of the girls, who were still too young and should never be left alone. I really couldn't work day or night while caring for them. I had been their babysitter from mid-December 2016 until then. I had to get busy a little to try to drown my regrets and resentments in a working environment.

But I remember that I had gone down to Bardamia the previous month, that is to say the day after the first hearing held on Friday, June 8th. It was on Saturday, June 9th that I left for the south. I had contacted Blanche by e-mail to express my imminent arrival and my desire to resume service the following Monday. She replied saying that I would have to go to her office on the Campus Seldom Secondary School to reactivate my registration with Golden Education Ltd., the company I had worked for since January 2006. I would be there from eleven o'clock on June 12th.

On that very day, I found myself with friends, the Notans, Adnan and Muriel. I had already put all my diplomas and other important documents in order and I was ready for my job interview. I was all dressed up in a dark suit and I was wearing a tie. It was a bit like back to school for me that bright and sunny day.

However, as I had a little time in front of me, I decided to check my e-mail box to check one last time the time of my meeting with Blanche. I found an e-mail that I had not read yet. I was coming from Stemar Bertrand, whom I knew full well and who was her hierarchical superior. I opened it and immediately I was flabbergasted by what I read there.

In a very terse message, Stemar was informing me that I was not welcome on their premises that day, or in the future for that matter as it had been brought to their attention that I had been arrested on suspicion of child abuse and neglect of my own children; and that, according to the law, they were no longer able to offer me either a job or an interview in order to find me one. I was hastily advised against even approaching their offices that day or in the future.

I did not know where I was. What planet was I on? Would I have descended on Mars or on the moon? I did not know if I was hot or if I was cold. My heart was pounding and my breath was racing. I was just suffocating. It was not possible ! What did I do to get here? Why was it that I was banned from the teaching profession and that I was immediately taken out of the classrooms that I had been attending in this country of Bingué for fifteen long years and counting, in addition to the eight previous years spent teaching in Ebrounia? How quickly did those people work? For a storm that rose in a cup of water last Thursday in Portalier, up north of Bingué, even the southern regions of the country were informed of my banishment from classes the following Monday? In just two working days, they managed to put an end to my career as an educator? And I had not had my say in all that?

I was completely dumbfounded. I did not know if the earth revolved around me or if it was rather me who had aggravated dizziness. Still, I was completely stunned by that brief email. I informed Adnan and Muriel who were just as dejected as I was.

- ''My God !'' they said. ''What do they want from you in the end? That you don't even work anymore? How do they want you to live then?'', they asked.

We simply did not have any answers to their questions. I sat down and tried to refresh my thoughts. There was something I definitely did not understand. I was sure there was something missing in all of this. I then remembered the dream that Claudia had had during Christmas 2016 in which Alesha had lined up my diplomas and degrees one after the other to sprinkle them with water. She sprinkled them with water while bearing a smirk on her face. In the dream, while Claudia reproached with her about her actions, she simply paid her no attention whatsoever.

When I became aware of that dream, I quickly understood that Alesha was determined to put an end to my career as an intellectual here in this country of Bingué. And if my diplomas were no longer of any use to me, I would henceforth be forced to work as some labourer in some factory or warehouse. As they say in Ebrounia, I would be forced to do *djossi* to survive – that is how we call the dirty and manual jobs that African migrants do in Bingué that do not require any qualification. The only problem was that that particular period was not auspicious to finding temporary work in that kind of industry. At the start of summer, everything was slowing down in factories and warehouses all across the country. For that reason, I had little chances of finding an unqualified job right away.

I thus found myself at a crossroads and I wondered what my choice should be for my immediate future. I decided that, since I would not be able to work in the field of education in the immediate future, there was no point in remaining in Bardamia, living with friends when I still had a semi-detached empty home in Portalier. I therefore decided to return there until the end of the school year and to participate in the July 4th hearing in court after which I would return to France and stay with my brother Jean-Baptiste for a while. I would wait there for the date of my departure for Ébrounia.

I returned to Portalier to remain in prayer and fasting until July 4th. I finally understood that the whole matter was more spiritual than material and that victory would only be achieved on my knees, in prayer and in fasting, and not in tribunals ran by humans. I began to understand that the spiritual dominated over the physical indeed thanks to all that God had put me through in terms of supernatural experiences. Still, I do not like much to talk openly about such things in front of do-gooders lest they would call me crazy. They just don't have any spiritual basis that would allow them to grasp spiritual matters. Many do not even believe in God in the first place. Besides, spiritual matters are not cut out for natural men, who are carnal in essence. They rather belong solely to spiritual men.

In the end, I went back to Portalier to fret my brakes. I no longer had children in my care. The house was empty and cold. Alesha and Lydia's room was desperately empty. Often times, I would go there to ask myself rhetorical questions. Why had Alesha made such serious accusations against me in the first place? What did she want in the end? At her age, where did she get such dark ideas from? Which demons were agitating her? Since when was she under the influence of the enemy to harm her own father like that? Why had her sister Lydia not defended me to the end? Why was she content to deny her sister's accusations only on the first day of the affair? Why did she not say anything more to continue to deny those false and senseless allegations? Were the girls happy where they were since June 7th? Did they at least miss me at all? Did they want to come home? Did they miss the real African meals they once ate? Where did they live? Were they really happier with complete strangers than with their father that I was? Was I as bad as Alesha claimed?

Some memories also came back to me like in 2014 when Alesha had spilled a kilogram of fine salt in the cooked sauce that was still on the cooker. Such level of salt was potentially capable of killing anyone who ate that meal. Luckily, her younger brother Darling had caught her pouring so much sodium chloride into the saucepan. I confronted her then to try to figure out what was on her mind when she carried out such a criminal action. She had no valid reason for doing so. I really worried about that then seven-year-old girl who had such deviant tendencies.

I also remember that I bought a kindle tablet from Amazon for each of the children: Darling, Alesha, Lydia and Karla. When Alesha dropped hers and smashed its screen by accident, I guess, she got revenge by damaging the other kids' tablets, cracking their screens too, so that she would not be alone with a damaged screen among several new and flawless tablets. Her brain has always worked backwards in gratuitous wickedness. Deep down in my daughter, there was a darkness whose origins I did not know, of course, but I suffered all its consequences as her brothers and sisters did too. Her mind was just twisted in many ways.

In May 2014, I accompanied some students from Daliville in France for a one-week school exchange. My French friend, Luc Descarpentes, who was the person who accommodated me back then, had given me a small racing car that moved by itself. He wanted me to give it to Darling who was a fan of cars and especially motor racing, Formula 1 and rallies of all kinds. Luc was also a rally driver in his spare time.

They both had a common passion for fast automobiles. Darling was very happy with his present until one day, unable to bear her brother's happiness much longer, Alesha deliberately stepped on the small car that was driving through the dining room. She simply crushed it to savour the pain the boy would experience. It was more than sadistic of her part. I can never forget the sad face of Darling when Alesha stepped on it to deliberately crush it. When I did confront her, she claimed it was all an accident! What else would she say? Alesha was always an accomplished and a compulsive liar. She would always be naughty and lie to you in your face.

In the days and weeks following my arrest and the first court hearing in Neuchastel, I truly sought God. Admittedly, without any rigorous methodology and know how because I did not know then the right method to seek God. I simply fasted regularly and prayed a lot. I prayed all the time and praised God. I read the Bible without meditating on the verses in writing. I had not learnt the written meditation at that point in time Still what is true is that I wanted to cooperate more with God who had warned me of so many dangers to come. I was looking for a much better intimacy with this benevolent God who always tipped me off before the big events in my life ever took place.

I remember precisely that he had also warned me of the death of my father, Seydou Bamba. First in 2010, he warned me that I wanted to do good to my dad who was a wicked man in the eyes of the Lord. For that reason, he told me back in the day that he would not benefit from my present. In 2012, I decided to build a house for my father in our native village, in Birgouin. I was accelerating the construction works of the house thinking that I could redeem the time and get ahead of God! It was pure madness on my part. When I had almost finished building the house, in December 2012, the Lord warned me that now that I had almost completed the construction works, I had to brace myself for the burial of my father because he would recall him in a month' time.

From that moment on every week I would ring my relatives back in the village to ask about my father's state of health. Lesner always told me he was doing fine. The third week, when I called my younger brother again, he told me that that time our dad was not really well. I immediately understood that my father was a dead man according to what my God had told me three weeks earlier. Right away, I offered to send money them the next day for Lesner to evacuate the old man to the hospital in Odelta. I thought I was still getting ahead of God and preventing, if possible, a certain death. It was still pure madness on my part again. My father himself strongly opposed such prospect of hospitalisation in Odelta on the grounds that his illness was not alarming enough to consider such an eventuality so soon. He proposed to stay in the village for at least a week. And, if he was not doing much better, then we could start the process of medical evacuation, which I reluctantly accepted.

But three days later, on January 19th, 2013, Lesner called me up after 8 p.m. Before picking up the call, I knew he would break the news that the old man had passed away. It was true. He had just left this world on the legs of my mother, the woman with whom he had shared nothing for past fourteen years. He no more ate the meals cooked by that hated woman nor would he wash with the hot water she offered him as they do in the village. Anyway, fate willed that it was she who took care of him in his last hours.

However, for the time being, I was unemployed here in Portalier. I no longer had a car since I decided to give up on my BMW X5 which was funded by a car finance company. I had paid up half of the 48 monthly repayments but given the current circumstances at the time, the five months spent in unemployment with no money coming in except from the welfare system, I was tired of clinging to that big 4X4 car. It was true that I had paid up over €6.000 in the past two years but I had two years of reimbursement left before becoming the rightful owner of the vehicle. It was simply not viable anymore to use my welfare handouts to repay that car loan company. I wanted more freedom: waking up every day without that feeling of having to put together €310 on a fixed date to pay up the monthly instalments. The car was therefore repossessed at my request in early April 2017 and sold at auction in less than five days. I was relieved on the spot but it was still madness to waste €6.000 on a car that I would not keep.

Since I no longer had a car, I had no choice but to go to the supermarkets on foot. I would go shopping and walk home with my parcels. It was tedious and I learnt to live without a car, to walk long distances to get to wherever I needed to go. Unemployed life is quite hard because you don't earn enough money every week like when I was teaching regularly. If I had kept my job, I could have kept my BMW X5 by accelerating the repayments to settle the balance within a year. The truth of the matter was that I was under tremendous pressure due to my unemployment. I had no other choice but to give up the car once and for all. To make things even worse, I had no more work of any kind anyway. The teacher that I was had been taken out of his class, and fast! I did not know at that time that I had signed a pact with unemployment for a long haul. I had not foreseen this low point of my life where even warehouses and factories were going to shut their doors before me and keep me at bay. Indeed, none of my job applications between June 2017 and June 2019 was even considered by any employer whatsoever. Both of them were blatantly ignored as if all the employers had conspired to boycott and starve me. I was at my wit's end. That was the saddest episode of my life.

The immediate consequence of that state of affairs was that I could no longer afford the luxury of taking up accommodation in Bingué. Certainly, if I did, Social Security would have paid up the rent for me as long as I was out of a job. I was a citizen of Bingué and had already worked in the country for several years. I had contributed to the economy of the country by paying my fair share of income taxes. I therefore had rights but I was no longer prepared to remain in the country like a parasite that did not work. I was rather sick and tired of sitting on my hands while the State would pay for my upkeep. I preferred to spend more time in Africa in order to grow in the Christian faith and to consider rebuilding my life from scratch other there. I wanted a fresh start in life.

Nonetheless, each time I happened to return to Bingué for a few months or weeks, my good friend Sonny had been kind enough to accommodate me. He did help me out throughout my entire journey through the desert and I owe him such a debt of gratitude that goes far beyond this lifetime.

Chapter 4

*The end of Police investigation does not mean that
I am out of the woods*

On August 6th, 2017, I was on vacation in Babiville, in my country of origin, in West Africa. I went to a cyber café to connect to the internet and check my emails. I received an e-mail that caught my attention: Morthuria Police informed me that they had completed their investigation into the allegations of abuse made by my daughter Alesha against me and that they had reached the conclusion that there was no conclusive evidence to support them. They had decided to close the case for good unless new evidence led them to reopen it. So, case closed! I heaved a sigh of relief. I knew it. I always knew it, from the first moment that affair broke out. I was sure that we would invariably come to that one conclusion: acquittal before even going to a trial before a magistrate.

My joy was therefore great knowing that the Morthuria Police had cleared me in that serious matter which had the potential of putting an end to my teaching career in Bingué. But I was under the illusion of thinking that I would finally be able to return to the binguist classes soon. I was making plans in my head for September 2017, because then I hoped to get back to work pretty soon afterwards. Again, it was madness on my part to think that way as I would soon understand. The sad truth was that I was far from out of the woods despite that dramatic development.

When I returned to Bingué in the first decade of September 2017, I realised that I was not out of the woods at all. Indeed, I found there an official letter from the CGE - General Council for Education -, which is the regulatory body for the teaching profession, or the equivalent of the Order of Teachers in certain countries. That body was informing me that I was suspended from my duties as a teacher in general secondary school education throughout the binguist territory until further notice. Reason for such a dramatic move: the CGE received a letter from the local authorities of Portalier informing it that a heavy suspicion weighed on me relating to child abuse, intentional assault and neglect. Those allegations were said to be based on the accusations of my daughter Alesha. Consequently, while waiting for an investigation by the CGE to come to an end, and to a happy conclusion which would eventually clear me of all suspicion, I am requested to no longer practice my teaching profession in any level of education on the binguist territory. I acknowledged the blow that just hit me hard but I did not understand anything anymore. The police cleared me of all suspicion in that very same case. That day, I was being cornered by the CGE which prevented me from teaching until further notice, exactly for the same file?

That was when I realised the season we were in. It was the autumn all around me: the trees planted in front of the house I was staying in, at Cottage Bruyère, were all without a shred of leaves. The branches that had become skeletal rose desperately in the air, swept in one direction then in another according to the wind which sometimes blew so hard in that month of September 2017. Those starving trees seemed to have vomited up their leftover brown leaves. Those leaves, precisely, littered the entire surface of the surrounding ground. It had become a challenge for all pedestrians of my kind as they stuck stubbornly to the heels and soles of the shoes. Most notably, in doing so, the dried leaves lessened the sound of the footsteps of anyone approaching us. This autumnal melancholy added to my despair and to my spite of the unfair system. I was suspended from all levels of teaching – from nursery to higher education - until further notice following a decision by the body of Bingué teachers! I was somehow made aware that such suspension was not a harbinger of guilt, far from it, simply rather a precautionary measure that was put in place to protect school children and pupils across the country until the administrative inquiry underway came to a final conclusion.

Regardless, I was suspended from all exercise of my profession until further notice. It's the only thing I remember and that profoundly tormented my mind for the few years ahead. What did I do to deserve such a fate? I could not sleep at night. In that room of mine, on the first floor, when I was lying in my bed, facing up towards the ceiling, I was drowning in my thoughts. What was that never ending case that kept unravelling? The four so white walls surrounding me dared not give me any answers. I was looking for answers and they unfortunately did not have any to provide me with. And I interrogated them time and again all night long without them volunteering to testify for or against me. Nor did the large glass windows on the far side of the walls dare leap to my defence either. If they were talking, what would those large glasses have to say in all that court case? And who would have believed them? The court judge? The accusers from the Council of Portalier? Would the social services working on behalf of the Council of Portalier accept their plea in my favour at all? My eyes remained fixed on the white ceiling and all night long I would wonder and question it. But this ceiling, as I expected, did not reply to me any more than the walls did and my head was boiling with all kinds of conjectures on the duration of such an administrative investigation, on its possible outcomes, on its pitfalls on my criminal record and therefore on its consequences on my teaching career.

The duvet cover on which I slept gave me no answers to those questions either, however essential to me they might have been. Even my beloved bed remained speechless in all that for it was where I encountered constant insomnia. My once faithful companion would harass me with its ardour and much stubbornness to keep me awake all night. My autumn nights were so sleepless, so heavy and so empty that I was dying of despair and hopelessness. I began to understand those who resorted to committing suicide in the face of certain trials in their lives. If I never really contemplated such extreme idea of taking my own life, it nevertheless did cross my mind from time to time. The autumn, the gloomy and morose weather, the ultimate time of spleen and death. Ah, that fall of 2017 was by far the saddest of them all for eighteen years! It was not only nature that was dying, out there beyond the large windows overlooking Cottage Bruyère here in Camembert with those bare trees which have become bald and suddenly sterile, but it was also and above all the unfortunate people who, like me, were dying slowly. Nothing is remotely so painful as a slow death here on this earth.

But, as a misfortune never comes round alone, I was looking for work elsewhere, in other industries, like in warehouses that offer so many thousands of jobs here in Bardamia, in Pierdrix County. We did not need academic qualifications to access those thousands of blue-collar jobs that struggled to be filled each year. The workforce was no longer so abundant in that autumn of 2017 because xenophobia has passed through the entire nation driving Eastern Europeans out. The political rhetoric of the demagogues' camp had never reassured the Eastern Europeans who had entered the EU since May 1st, 2004. There had been much talk of upcoming expulsions concerning them and several thousands of them volunteered to head back to their home countries.

However, I was seriously mistaken because even in the many warehouses where I applied for an unqualified job, I got absolutely nothing in return. No one deigned to answer me or to offer me a job interview. Everywhere I was ignored. Soon enough I had the clear impression that I no longer existed at all. Even for the *djossi* - this is how we call the unskilled jobs that African migrants gladly accept to do, killing themselves by carrying out two or three full-time jobs all at once -, there was nothing left for me. I, who had always looked down on those jobs because of my PhD and my title as a doctor, I was merely reduced to begging in vain for a position as an operative in the many binguist warehouses without the slightest success! The relentlessness of fate on me led me to think that that particular case was not only a mere legal matter but rather did it have a spiritual overtone. I had the impression that all doors were closed before me, at least all doors of employment in land of Bingué.

I crossed my fingers and hoped that soon enough the CGE would clear my name of all suspicion and that I would once again be allowed to go back to schools and practice the profession that I embraced from a very young age. The truth was that I would need a lot of patience before that happened. I had to return to Ebrounia several times in a row between July 2017 and April 2019. Those trips allowed me to enjoy changes in environments and cultures. I was a permanent tourist in Ebrounia and in Bingué and that certainly helped to survive my ordeal.

I was totally unemployed on both sides of the Atlantic and the situation had become burdensome. In another dream, in January 2019, I saw that I had won a great victory over Alesha and I understood then that I was undoubtedly close to the end of the tunnel. On January 9th indeed, I received a letter from the General Council of Education informing me that my suspension from the teaching profession had been lifted. The body detailed its investigation and the interviews it had carried out, the material evidence it had requested and had not obtained. The traces of caning that Alesha spoke of did not exist. The accuser's DNA had not been found on any of my belts. The medical examinations carried out on her and her sister Lydia by three consultant paediatricians at the Neuchastel hospital on June 7th, 2017 had uncovered no proof of ill-treatment on any of the girls. Generally speaking, the three specialists who examined them could not establish that they bore any signs of domestic abuse.

From all the above reasons, I only retained that I had won a spiritual victory over Alesha as my God had announced to me a week before the arrival of the CGE letter. I breathed a real sigh of relief that day but I had already bought my flight ticket to Babiville for a three months' stay starting on January 16th. So, I had to leave for Africa for three months as planned. Anyway, had I wished to rush back into classrooms across the County, I would have had to get a new criminal record established beforehand. That process would take up to twelve weeks to complete.

While I was in Ébrounia, I met the CMFI which was to become my true religious community from then on. It made me really progress in the faith and in spiritual matters in general. They preached to me that clear Gospel which saves lives. I loved the gospel that was preached to me in that church so much so that I became seriously attached to it. I was led to repentance and was baptised by immersion once again. I also went through the process of deliverance as it is customary to the CMFI.

When the time of my stay was over, I returned to Londamou on April 16th, 2019 to introduce a formal criminal record application in order to resume my profession. I had to wait to get it and it was only on August 6th that I received it. It was as clean and white as snow. No crime was recorded there, not even traces of any arrest or of any police warning whatsoever. I was truly over the moon. On that day, I understood what the words born again really meant. I was born again, born to life, born again to be a teacher. Another Goliath had fallen. I could then consider life under better auspices. I had hope again. I then understood that hope means a lot of things in the life of a human being. Without hope, we no longer live; we barely survive with air in our lungs. Nothing more. With hope, comes back the taste for life, projects, perspectives, ambition, in short, humanity comes back galloping like a racing horse. I had become a human being once again and not just a mass that moved in the crowds which no one could see. I was no longer irrelevant.

I then understood that sometimes human life hangs by a thread. It is often said as an apt expression among many others but we don't necessarily realise what that means. It simply means that an unforeseen and a sudden event can turn your life upside down to a level that surprises and shakes you to the core of your inner being. Your whole life can then capsize like a boat tossed here and there by the winds and the gigantic waves of the ocean. On that morning of June 7th, 2017, I had made breakfast for my daughters: coffee with milk, with Nesquick, eggs and toast. They had had a good breakfast and my son Joshua had accompanied them to school. I had no idea what was happening behind the scenes at their school that day. At two o'clock, I went into the kitchen to prepare their evening meal as usual. That day, on the menu, alloco – a dish from our home in Ebrounia -, French fries, a chili vinaigrette, Heinz sauce and baked chicken thighs. All was set and I was looking forward to seeing my girls come home and enjoy their meal. I never thought they would not be coming home neither that evening nor on any other day for the next six years or more. I was clearly mistaken in thinking that they would enjoy what I cooked for them when they got home. Clearly, they did not return that evening. They never actually came back. It has been six years since they last returned from school. They never called me on the phone either from that day on. I never saw them again. They are somewhere out there. Never would I have imagined that my quiet life as a law-abiding citizen could have been turned upside down that much.

For someone like me that lived with eight children under the same roof up until November 2016, with my wife, a happy family of ten individuals, I saw the empire that I had built collapse all around me. I had fought hard so that the three children I had had by other women – Joshua, Alesha and Lydia – could all come and live with my wife and me here in Bingué so that they would all treat her like their mother. I wanted them all to feel equal. I wanted to give each of them the same chance to succeed in life by getting a better education and upbringing. I wanted them all to live in the same social and family conditions, etc. I thought that was equal opportunity at work but I was clearly and badly mistaken. Alesha had a different agenda to mine and she was determined to ruin everything I had built up to that point in time.

Generally, I would say that two unexpected events overturned this whole paradigm of my settled family life. First on Sunday, June 12th, 2016 with Kyria's shocking revelations about the sixteen years of marital infidelity caused a first deep fracture in the family unit. On November 11th, 2016, I made the decision to leave the marital home to go with Alesha and Lydia who were not born to my wife. Joshua was already of age at eighteen and was pursuing his psychology studies at the University of Abertune, north of Gailla.

However, the second event that was to shatter everything else was undoubtedly the slanderous denunciation by Alesha on June 7th, 2017. On that fateful same day, I was alone in the world. I no longer had a wife. I no longer had any children living with me. I was alone. All alone. Completely alone in the world. The house was big, far too big for me. A semi-detached house with three good sized bedrooms and a large living room downstairs, with a sizeable kitchen. There was a garden behind the house which was fully fenced up. It was in that garden that the two police cars parked before picking me up from the house to drive me to the central police station. I owed such an upheaval in my life to my nine-year-old daughter: Alesha. I was arrested and handcuffed in front of my nineteen-year-old son, in my living room, in broad daylight, at around three forty-five minutes. It was total infamy. The worst humiliation I had to endure in my whole life. I know that I made terribly poor decisions because I was so angry at the turn of events that unfolded back then. The most terrible decision I made was to withdraw altogether from the legal proceedings after the second hearing. That was yet another folly of which I sincerely repent nowadays. I should have played the game out until the end. They would eventually return my children to me, after six months or more. There would be no other avenue opened for them but to return my girls to me albeit under the close supervision of the social services.

I can only speculate on the state of mind of my son Joshua who witnessed my arrest. He has seen it all. In front of him, I had to stretch both my arms forward, so that one of the policemen took out his handcuffs and tied my wrists together. He didn't squeeze them very hard. Apparently, he felt troubled by the necessity to chain me up like that in my rental house, me, a PhD holder, in front of my nineteen-year-old student son. He even asked me if the handcuffs were comfortable enough, otherwise he would loosen them up some more. But how can one ever be comfortable in chains? I thought that only the Kunta Kintes or demons suffered such fate, but not me, the intellectual; not me, the doctor with a PhD, a long-time serving teacher! Not me the law-abiding citizen! However, there I was, in chains, by the evil will of my daughter Alesha, who came to Bingué at the age of three to torment and humiliate me to the depths of my humanity. I was in chains as I had often read in French literary works by the likes of Jean-Jacques Rousseau and Alexandre Dumas. I was in chains. Yes, it was not a dream, not even a nightmare. I was really in chains. And it was real. I was in chains and I was leaving my house in cuffs, between two policewomen who flanked me right and left. I was under arrest. I was in chains. How did my son experience and process that scene? I never knew. We never talked about it. It was the law of the omerta. We acted like it never happened. Someone said that great pains are silent. It was most likely true. In any case, I concede it to them as mine was ever so silent too.

PART TWO

THE WORLD AS IT STOOD WHEN WE WERE CHILDREN

Chapter 1

The happy ending of my secondary school education

However, I remember as if it were yesterday, the year 1988 when I was still a student in my final year of secondary school education back in Africa. I was attending the modern high school of Odelta and I was head of the class. I was rather a brilliant student in that class of thirty-one students, all of whom had successfully passed the so feared probationary baccalaureate for the year 1987. It comes back to me that I was ranked third in the first semester out of the thirty -one students with an average mark of 12 out of 20. In the second semester, I was ranked second out of the total number with an annual average of 12.31 out of 20. Bakayoko Sékou was the only one ranked above me mainly because of his brilliant averages in non-essential subjects such as mathematics and to a lesser degree, because he was one of the few students in the class to come out on top in the old grammatical concepts of Gouro Bi Dandy, our English teacher and his assessments drawn exclusively from his unpublished novels written in English, which no one had ever read except himself. I admit that I did not understand anything about his grammatical concepts of the English language. Before he became my teacher, I was always among the two best students in English but suddenly, I found myself at the tail end with an average of 06 out of 20. Nonetheless, I never doubted my abilities in the language of Shakespeare because I had been brilliant during the mock baccalaureate exam in March 1988. Moreover, during the real baccalaureate exam in June, I had chosen, without hesitation, English as first choice living language which went with a coefficient of 4 for the written exam paper and 3 for the oral one, i.e. granted it a cumulative coefficient of 7 out of 25. I remember very well having done the right choice because I got 16/20 in the oral English exam and 13/20 in the written one. Given the high coefficients, I got 48 marks and 52 points respectively, i.e. 100 points out of 250 required to pass the baccalaureate. That meant that my baccalaureate was more than assured. All my concern turned to obtaining it with honours.

It is true that if my English grades were bad in class with my teacher, mister Gouro Bi, those of French with Mr. Bandeloquent were excellent because I was top of the class in his subject with 13.41 out of 20. I was in the top three in Spanish with a similar annual average mark. I was also among the top three in history and geography with over 14 out of 20. In philosophy, I was still ranked second with more than 12 out of 20. If we limited ourselves to the so-called essential subjects, I was consistently better ranked than Sékou. Mathematics and English version Gouro Bi put him a little above me at the end of the year, but only by a very short head.

I remember that I was a young man full of confidence in my intellectual abilities at that time. I was convinced that nothing could stop me, intellectually speaking. Throughout the school year, I was spoilt for choice following my success at the baccalaureate. My heart told me to do a law degree while I had a real enthusiasm for English. Moreover, I had the fascination of the proselyte for philosophy. Socrates and Plato were like personal friends to me and I loved them to bits. I truly loved philosophizing. I was keen on reading and mastering all the writing techniques for all subjects combined. I was also excellent in French and I was a real disciple of my first-class French teacher, Mr. Coulibaly Djakaridja. I was rightfully top of the class in his subject. I was also top of the class in my final year under a different teacher. I rightfully wanted to carry on studying French literature as well.

After obtaining the baccalaureate A2 in Philosophy-Literature series with brilliance, I finally chose to study literature at the ENS - École Normale Supérieure in Babiville - to graduate as a French teacher. My choice was more guided by the attractiveness of the scholarship which amounted to 60,000 f.cfa per month. That was an awful lot of money for the poor man's son that I was. It was indeed an unexpected financial windfall for us, children of farmers and moreover, the ENS guaranteed us the status of civil servants directly employed by the ministry of national education. In addition, there was that peculiar pride of being recruited directly at the ENS after the baccalaureate since the conditions of enrolment at that college were the toughest and the most selective of them all. The students from the ENS had that pride and that feeling of being among the brightest in their class because they could each boast of having surpassed the average of 12 out of 20 in their core subject. That average was worked out as the average of the annual class work combined with the grade obtained during the national baccalaureate exam. Out of the three thousand high school graduates in Ebrounia in the year 1988, only 204 had thus successfully made it to the ENS in Literature series. I felt privileged in a way to be one of them.

It is true that the 1987-1988 school year was the happiest of my school life. I had finally overcome my great shyness due to the stuttering that I had experienced in my childhood. I had become a class leader and was in constant contact with both my classmates and with all of our teachers. I confidently and competently helped them prepare their book of records. Everything was always in order and neat, without erasure. They were all proud of me and my academic performance as a class leader. I felt comfortable in class in all subjects, except probably in mathematics where I had no more than 09 out of 20. That was my only weak point. I had no other weaknesses. Even in P.E. which was not my strongest point, I had at least 12 out of 20. I led by example of hard work well done. I was pretty good a class leader. That is why, that year, the one mile or so that separated the home of my guardian, Lall Sidibé, in the Texas neighbourhood of Odelta from the modern high school of the city seemed to me a sweet torment. I walked them with great happiness every day there and back, knowing that I walked that distance with great happiness every day back and forth for the seventh and last year of my life. I was convinced that the following school year, I would be in Babiville, the economic capital of the country, to pursue higher education either at the University of Cocody or at the ENS of Babiville.

I had likewise learnt to love and cherish the hours spent working in the shallows where my guardian grew rice. I loved working in its eight plots with songs of joy knowing that it was for the very last year of my life. I had even forgotten the work accident that had happened to me on Sunday, January 18th, 1987 in that same place. The sharp machete I was holding on that fateful Sunday had ricocheted off a stubborn clump of grass and sliced through my left leg. It sectioned my hamstring muscle in that leg. In the initial thirty seconds or so, I had not really felt any pain in spite of my flesh being lacerated by the machete that was sharpened the night before. The spectacle I witnessed back then unfolded as follow : I saw the skin of my left leg cut open on nearly eight centimetres long. The red flesh was open. The hamstring muscle was completely severed. I could see my shin with my naked eyes. It was all white. For a second or two, maybe even almost a minute, there had been no bloodshed whatsoever. I was amazed at the surreal scene I saw but then the blood suddenly began to spurt out like an ox that had just been slaughtered. I was not fooled. I remembered the biology lessons I had taken over the past years. I knew that a few minutes would have been enough for me to lose all my blood and my life along with it. I knew that I needed a clean cloth to apply a tourniquet to my leg. I did not find anything around me. I immediately understood my predicament : the bleeding had to be stopped immediately, without delay, by all means and at all costs. So, I took a smelly clod from the shallows to apply it to the wound. I plugged the gaping hole with this filthy mud and tied it all together with a piece of dirty cloth picked up nearby. I just ensured the mud would not fall off and the blood start pouring out again. My life was at stake and I did not entertain the idea of losing it at the tender age of almost seventeenth. In fact, I was one month shy of turning seventeen on that sad day.

I even forgot that on that fateful Sunday, there was no doctor at Odelta General Hospital. There was just that male nurse who was on duty. He treated me in the worst possible way. He scolded me for having had the terrible idea of stopping the bleeding with some shallow mud. He was further incensed by my poor judgment in having used some random dirty old piece of cloth to bandage the wound. He truly was in a bad mood as he superficially cleaned the wound with mercurochrome and alcohol before applying local anaesthesia to the left leg. He then performed on me three levels of suture. The very low level was in the depths of my flesh, near the tibia, then another one was done halfway, above the first one and then the third level of suture was performed at the skin level. At that stage, I was suffering terribly and I almost cried out. The nurse scolded me further and screamed saying that I was not feeling anything since I was under local anaesthesia. Why was I screaming then? If he knew that I was in terrible agony indeed and my cries were enough evidence of that reality.

He released me some three-quarters of an hour after my arrival at the hospital. Shockingly enough, by the next day, on Monday January 19th, 1987, I had become a crippled young man who was completely unable to walk. I was disabled as I was restricted to dragging myself on the ground like a hemiplegic young fella to move from point A to point B. I remember that that very Monday, I had to go to the school infirmary to inform the local medical services of my state of health. They had to start from scratch the whole work carried out by the nurse who had seen me the day before at Odelta hospital. He had treated me just one day before but the wound already smelled of gangrene; it had the smell of some rotten meat. My flesh was spoiled by the filthy mud of the shallows as the nurse failed to clean it sufficiently before giving me the three layers of stitches. Everything had to be undone, thread by thread, from the skin on the surface to the bone of the tibia in depth. The skin had already solidified, however. After a deep cleaning, it had become almost impossible to redo the suture as the skin had stretched several centimetres from bottom to top. All they could do was to treat the wound and bandage it in the hope it would eventually heal.

I still had thirty days of incapacity for work. I would therefore remain grounded during this time, dragging my body on the ground like a paralytic old man. I truly understood then that everything is grace here below. Walking on your feet is a grace that is not granted to everyone out there. I was under seventeen and yet I was crippled and unable to walk. There was no doubt I learned at that time to be content with what I had : some air in my lungs and breathing without artificial assistance; my full eyesight; walking on my legs without assistance; hearing sounds distinctly and smelling odours. Everything is grace here below because there are only healthy people who are mad enough on earth to ask God for something else. Only the sick and the wounded know the true meaning of life : they ask only for perfect health and nothing more. Keeping the integrity of one's physical body is the most important thing on earth because everything else is merely an add-on gift. I had completely lost my appetite. I could only enjoy drinking water for the entire first week. I needed just water, all the time, again and again, to try to control an unquenchable thirst. I then realised that mankind could eventually survive a long while without food but certainly not without water for water is probably the most valuable commodity here on earth.

However, after a month spent at home, during which time I never went to school, I had sharply fallen behind in all disciplines. I had missed entire chapters in mathematics, in physics, in biology and in philosophy. I have never copied the lessons I had missed since 1987 to date. On February 13th of that year, I thus learned that on February 18th the mock exam of the probationary baccalaureate would take place. I absolutely wanted to measure myself on that real scale to assess my chances of success in the final exam which was the most feared in the country. Scores of Ebrounian students had to circumvent it by going abroad to study in the neighbouring Fasso where that exam did not exist. That way, they would go directly to the final year of secondary school education and most often they would successfully pass their baccalaureate in that country and return home quietly to continue their higher education in our national University of Babiville or in our Higher Education Institutions.

On the day of the mock exam, I was taken to the exam rooms on a motorbike by a friend of mine, Doumbès Bacchus, who had dropped out of school altogether a year before. He had taken me to school on my guardian's motorbike. Somehow, without having revised the slightest lesson for a month, without even having taken the time to copy out the new lessons that I had missed in the previous thirty days, I still managed to rise to second best position in my class in the literature series which included two classrooms totalling seventy-two students. Only Gouléon Lizazon Gérard did beat me to the top spot. He was the only one who passed the mock exam with an average of 10 out of 20. I followed him with 179 points where 180 marks would have allowed me to pass it too. It was such a blow that hit me hard on the chin because I had failed that mock exam by merely one point. It was true that in all the core subjects I did really well by getting good grades. Only the marks in mathematics, physics and biology were catastrophic : the tests had focused mainly on the last chapters my comrades had studied while I was out of school through my horrible injury. And, of course, I did not even know the title of those chapters!

It was with great hope however that I looked forward to my certain success in the national examination which would take place in June 1987. I always believed that a so-called large-scale national examination was designed for the average candidate to pass, not for geniuses or gifted ones. In fact, in the first semester of this year, I was top of my class. I was ranked top student in French, second in English, second in philosophy, second in Spanish, first in history and geography. I was not bad in physics and in biology either as I had claimed the average of 11 out of 20 in each of them. In mathematics, I only had 09 out of 20 in the first semester, before the fateful accident which was to keep me away from classes for a month.

It is true that in the second semester, I never knew how to catch up in certain scientific subjects. That drastically reduced my general second semester average but I did secure the general annual average. Most reassuringly, I had not dropped in any of the core literary subjects. It was therefore with ease that I passed my probationary baccalaureate in June 1987.

Basically, the first and final classes of the secondary school were the easiest classes for me, the ones where I had the most fun. I had finally grown in confidence and I was brilliant without working too hard nor forcing my talent. I did not really study much although I did read the few novels that I could to get my hands on. I usually devoured them in three full days at most whether it was *Germinal* by Émile Zola with its 503 pages or *Tribaliques* by Henri Lopès. I was always aware that in my school career I never used more than ten percent of my intellectual abilities.

I remember that was the moment where I fell in love with Bella Mader. She was a young girl enrolled in year eight in 1985-86 while I was in year ten. She was my sweetheart but I was just too shy to approach her and chat her up. Her class leader, Savané Moussa, was a good friend of mine. We were both from the district of Tielma. No doubt Savané had spilled the beans to her because she knew all along that I secretly in love with her although I never spelt it out.

It was the following year when I was in year eleven and that she was in year nine that I finally had the courage to declare my love for her. I was a little more extrovert by then. I was top of my class and I could handle myself a little bit better. Of course, she had nothing to do with me as she was already the girlfriend of her English teacher, Sidy Conardou, a dandy and a narcissistic fella. He had taken her virginity for a while already and had even found her a rival since he was also dating Nouma Farria, the beautiful and lovely daughter of some singing star of the West of the country, Farria Peter. The two girls were in the same class and the battle was tough between them. Bella still managed to throw her rival from the love triangle relationship. I pursued her with all my ardour all the same until my final year at school. She was then in year ten but I had no chance of being in a relationship with her as long as she was with that young English teacher. Those people passed for snobs who mystified us because they taught English, an exotic language. I now know that they did not really know much about English anyway. After a few years spent in Bingué, when I came back to the country of my birth and I spoke the language with those English teachers, they could not hold a dissent conversation. When we watched DVDs of American films together, they understood almost nothing in the dialogues and were surprised that I could understand everything that those American actors were saying. I measured their limits and understood that they had mystified us for far too long.

Overall, I really liked my high school. It was built on a large flat land, several acres of absolutely flat land. There were eight buildings combined in pairs, which made it look like there were four buildings instead of eight. Each building included three large classrooms downstairs and upstairs, six rooms per individual building and twelve rooms per paired buildings. Some rooms served as laboratories for the natural and physical sciences. The year seven students took a building twinned with that of the year eights. The year nine students used another building, the other side of which was dedicated to the year tens. The year eleven students shared their twin buildings with the year twelve students. The seniors had their separate building. The educators of each level held offices in the building of the level for which they were responsible, which was suitable and convenient to everyone.

There was behind the building of the year thirteen students the refectory for the boarding school pupils who exceeded the four hundred students each year. Beyond that, there were the two buildings in the background which served as a dormitory for the boarding school boys. Those of the boarding school girls were directly opposite as we progressed towards the main administrative building where the Headteacher and his deputies had their offices as well as the other school officials, namely the school Bursar and the Educational Advisor. All those buildings were painted in beige. They were not really yellow but not really white either. The high school had been offered to the city of Odelta in 1972 when the rotating independence was celebrated in the city during the golden age of the reign of Nanafouè Borgna. There were paved roads everywhere throughout the school. I loved my high school and my career there had had a very happy ending, even without the love of the beautiful Bella Mader.

Chapter 2

Memories of my melancholic childhood in the village

In October 1974, the young teacher Lamdan Badoum was assigned to my village in Birgouin to run the new public primary school that had just been built there. Let us just say a building with three classrooms was standing tall on the school ground. And, for that young teacher who had just left the Cafop, the primary school teachers' training school, it would be the baptism of fire because he was the only teacher in the school and he would be his own Headteacher with no other collaborators.

The villagers were sceptical of the intrusion of Western education into their way of life. No one wanted to enrol their son at school, let alone their daughter. Everyone needed instead their children to help them in the farms. Early on, the older people in the village challenged my father, Salman Bamba, urging him to provide students for the new school on the grounds that he had many children! He complied and registered me as the very first student enrolled at our village school. I was not the darling child of my father, far from it, and was therefore expendable. In my dad's mind, I was fit to rot on the school benches. The teacher Lamdan was glad that he had his very first student, me, Fabien Bamba, but he wanted more. Some surrounding villages which had not yet hosted any schools were coming to our rescue : Varna, Missamba and Kongofila. Despite all the great effort made by the four villages, the numbers were still very low. Since the harvest was nowhere near good enough, the villagers once again put pressure on my father, who was only thirty-seven at the time, urging him once more to provide more children to fill the class of year one because he had a much larger family. He reluctantly added my youngest brother, Yamis, who was enrolled in the same class as me.

In total, we were about twenty children enrolled in year one when classes began on Friday, October 18th, 1974. Everything was going well generally speaking and my big sister, Marya, was more than willing to go to school. She joined us for all the activities, including the schoolyard weeding with machetes and hoes commonly called *dabas*. Under no circumstances my dad would allow her to get an education. He would come and forcibly withdraw her from our midst every day and make her join my mother, Maya Tamara, in the kitchen. She was made to understand more than once that school was not a woman's business but rather a man's affair. It was such a pity as Marya was clearly intelligent and ever so motivated and eager to get an education. After a few weeks of trying hard, she abandoned her ambition and quit the ranks of students on roll.

We boys carried on attending school until the first assessment came about. I remember I was ranked third or fourth out of the twenty or so students in my class. At the end of the year, I moved on to year two like the others. But at the end of 1976, everything went wrong : Mister Lamdan abruptly left the village without notice. It was such a hasty exit that rumours went round suggesting that he had had an illicit sexual relationship with a married woman in the village and that he felt threatened by her jealous husband. Anyway, it happened that he never returned to the village for the start of the 1976-1977 school year when we were due to start year three.

He got finally replaced by a new teacher, mister Diomansy, who would immerse himself in the village life by becoming a formidable hunter during bushfires. He would even turn out to be a panther killer. Since he did not know the students and their ability, he could only ask who worked hard enough to progress to year three class. Those who were supposed to repeat year two were asked to stand in the left corner while the one that made it to year three were asked to stand in the right corner of the classroom. Naturally, I joined those who were moving up to year three class although the older boys tried hard to expel me from their midst on the grounds that I was too small a boy to join them. They tried to intimidate and bully me but I fiercely refuse to budge. I stood up to them knowing that I did not want to repeat year two. Again, I knew very well that I was one of the best students in year two the previous academic year. Finally, mister Diomansy decided and I could stay in year three. When the first term assessment came round in early December 1976, I was glad I beat most of the big boys who wanted to kick me out of that year three class at the start of the school year. I must say that school was never really difficult for me. I even found it easy because even though I did not really take time to revise my lessons, I always got good grades. I was content to concentrate in class and listen carefully to the explanations given by the teacher. That was how I went from class to class until year six in 1981 when the first students from our school in Birgouin went to secondary school in Odelta. I was very excited to be part of the pioneer cohort of five students that attended high school that year. Fate later on appointed me as one of the first two, with Kondy Balkar, to pass the general secondary school education certificate, the BEPC or the GCSE in Bingué in 1985. I was fifteen years old at the time.

The same fate would make me the first high school graduate from that primary school in 1988 when I passed my baccalaureate. Also, I turned out to be the first student from my village to pursue higher education. I was the very first *normalien* - and the first to become a secondary school teacher - from my village and from that primary school founded in 1974. I would also become the first graduate, the first postgraduate, the first one to obtain a DEA and to hold a PhD in 2003. Of course, in 1985, when I passed the BEPC, I had no idea whatsoever I had a pioneering role that I would always have to assume going forward.

In the village, I liked to go to the fields at weekends although I was not a champion in farm work. I have always worked better with my head rather than with my muscles and hands. I still worked well in the fields, methodically, but my overall performance in terms of area covered was lower than that of my younger brother, Yamis. I never wanted to compete with anyone in farm work, but when it came to formal education, I made a point of staying at the top of the rankings. I did not accept being ranked at the bottom of the table nor even in mid-table.

What I liked most about going to the fields was to admire nature, especially the trees along the rivers where nature was more luxuriant and the vegetation closer to the forest landscapes. I loved the greenery of the grass and the cries of the crickets and other insects that swarmed in the open fields. I liked to hear the breeze sweeping the foliage of the trees and gently swaying the branches left and right and back and forth as if cradling a baby. Oh, yes, the shade of the trees also fascinated me as I always hated the scorching heat of the sun in the Odelta region which regularly peaked at 36°C. I believe that that early childhood prepared me for the binguist adventure when I was around twenty-nine. I always sought shade from the trees on my way to the farms as it made the seven kilometres walk much easier to handle.

When I was between three and four years old, I remember my father used to take us on his bicycle, Yamis and me, to go to the farm. Yamis and I were not helping with farm work at the time. We just sneaked through the grass behind our father and visited the traps he set for wild animals. If there was any trapped prey in any of the snares, it was good food that day. Bushmeat, as it is called in Ebrounia, is very popular with us. It has a particular taste and makes sauces really appetising. I remember that at that time, and the years that followed, I had developed a certain honesty that led me to always assume my actions and to accept their consequences, whatever they might have been.

One day, when I was about seven years old – it was around 1977 - my older brother, Adam, started throwing stones at Fatima, the daughter of Birahim Colou, the biggest merchant in the village. Yamis and I followed suit. We stoned her too but our projectiles could not go very far to harm her since she was standing at a considerable distance from us. Adam however was always a dexterous child who would prove his natural ability throughout his adult life by becoming a real hunter, a *dozo* as we call the hunters' fellowship. He would indeed follow in the footsteps of our father in that elite group much later on. Coming back to our initial story, he threw yet another stone that hit the little girl on the head. She screamed in agony and we fled the scene. Her blood was gushing out and obviously it was pretty serious by the look of it.

Her dad had naturally complained to ours about our reprehensible behaviour. Our father was therefore waiting for us to teach us a lesson meaning a beating worthy of our crime. We were informed of his resolution and refused to go home until bedtime. We were hungry because the incident had happened in the morning and up until bedtime, we had not been able to make it to enjoy either our lunch nor our dinner. It was already almost nine o'clock and we had still not had a bite at anything. As we all had cramps in our empty stomachs, I resolved to go home and accept whatever punishment that was in store for me out there. My brothers thought I was nuts for wanting to go home as it was certain that dad would hit me hardest.

Nevertheless, I would rather go home and get punished right away. The headlong rush would get us nowhere because after all we would end up going home sooner or later. Besides, no matter how long it would take, I remained convinced that dad would not hesitate to punish us whenever we returned home. When I came home alone that evening, he called me up and scolded me before I was whipped. Though I was less badly beaten up than I thought I deserved. After all, a little girl my age had had her head pierced, as they said, and she had lost a lot of blood. My father had given me three lashes, not one more. I screamed as if I were being slaughtered but that was rather out of fear of being beaten up than out of sheer agony and pain. My father let go of me and soon I was allowed to eat my meal. I congratulated myself then on having made the right decision to go home first and to being handed out my punishment first.

It must be said that we feared our father greatly. We were frankly afraid of him although he did not beat us often. He would rather harshly scold us. I do not remember him beating me more than three times in my entire life. He seemed stern with us, his children, although he was a very jovial man with those from outside his family. He joked happily with the other children in the village who loved to play and joke with him so much. But for us, he was the absolute authority. It was dad, a very austere and a very strict dad who never had normal conversations with any of us. We never joked with him either. He spoke to us only to give orders, directions, instructions or to send us an errand. Those were our sole talks.

However, what made me sad was that out of his three wives, my mother was the only one he always beat up. The only one I ever saw him beating up was her. I was too young to understand their adult arguments and I do not know if my mother disrespected him more than anyone else or if he simply loved her less than her rivals. The fact of the matter is that I saw him scolding her violently on several occasions. I could see that she was terrified of him. Sometimes he whipped her in front of everyone in the mornings. She then had to flee and spend a few hours with neighbours until his anger faded away.

But the one incident that really upset me was that one morning, at around nine o'clock, he started whipping my mother again. In her flight, her loincloth had fallen off. She dared not go back to pick it up and tie it up. It was a humiliation for her and a source of bitterness for my soul. I wondered why my father behaved like that with her and why she was singled out for such beatings and humiliations.

Almost forty years later my mother remembered that inglorious period of her life and told me that my late father had stopped beating her after a few years for a reason. He had overheard a conversation between two women in the village who did not know that he was close to them and could hear everything they said to each other about him. So, the two women were criticising him saying that he had beaten up yet again his wife Maya, my mother. In essence, they were saying that he battered her almost every other day or so and that even the day before, at breakfast time, he had badly battered her again. They criticised him in inglorious terms because he had never raised a hand on any other of his wives, not even against the one that had so openly humiliated him by cheating on him for a whole year, making him the laughing stock of the entire village. Nevertheless, he had never raised hands on her. The women claimed my father was ever so eager to beat the hell out of my mother, guilty or innocent, to appease his guilty conscience. My father, having heard those harsh words condemning him as an unjust man, did not come out of his hiding place. He was ashamed of himself and realised how much the whole village was criticising him like those two although no one took their courage to say it in his face.

Anyway, growing up, I was well aware of the fact that my father did not really like my mother. It was obvious at first glance. Everyone knew he loved Ndèye, his true darling, the youngest of his three wives and the love of his life. She could do no wrong. She was always right in anything she did. I never heard my father reprimand her until the day he died on January 19th, 2013. I never saw him argue with her either. He never whipped her. It was almost the same for Najat, the first wife.

Likewise, I knew very well that I was not his favourite son. It was probably for that reason that he enrolled me at school first. As paradoxically as that may seem, he thought he was getting rid of me that way. The others could stay with him to help him out in his farm work. It was on the insistence of the other villagers that he resolved to enrol Yamis at school in addition to me.

Besides, he wasn't the only one who hated me in the family. I knew his mother, my grandmother, Sérida Damsouba, hated me much more than he did. My father had at least the finesse to save appearances. His hatred for me was veiled and he could motivate and articulate it : I was not good a farmer like my other two brothers, Adam and Yamis. Thus, he would eat his meat and share it with the latter as incentive for working hard in the fields. In our tradition, the meat in the sauce exclusively belongs to the eldest person around the table, or should I say around the saucepan. He always said that my brother had earned the right to eat meat with him for working hard on his farms. I gladly accepted that explanation although I thought he should have had a much better rating criterium. We were both enrolled in school. So, since we were students, I thought whoever did best in class deserved to be rewarded, which was never the case. I never got any present whatsoever when I passed my SATs exam nor did I get one when I passed my GCSEs. I never got rewarded either when I passed my A-levels nor when I qualified as a teacher. The same thing happened again when I passed my postgraduate degrees and my doctorate.

My grandmother's detestation was more visible and more vocal though. She never hid it as she was less of a diplomat. However, I truly loved my father and my grandmother from the bottom of my heart. My great worry was that my grandmother would eventually die before I became a civil servant. That would prevent me from offering her the significant present I was so desperate to get her before her death. Alas, in September 1991, while I was a young trainee teacher, she passed away aged 104. It was the most painful mourning I had to endure in my entire life because I wanted to shower her with gifts in her lifetime. Sadly enough, she left the scene one month before I started working for the government as a civil servant. Of all the one hundred and twenty-one grandchildren and great-grandchildren she had on the day of her passing, grandmother only summoned Yamis alone, my youngest brother, to come see her on her deathbed back in the village before her final departure. She wanted to see him and him alone. We, the others, did not count in his eyes.

In spite of all the above, I loved my father so much that I never blamed him for anything. I had always preferred him to my mother probably out of gender solidarity. Whenever I had money to give my parents, I irretrievably and invariably gave it to my father and my mother always complained about it. I understood much later that he never gave my mother a penny, ever. Foolishly enough, I even had the guts to reprimand my mother saying that my father had a lot more responsibilities than her as head of the family. He had to take the money and take care of his entire family according to priorities. I thought it was up to him to manage the financial windfall that fell into his hands for the benefit of the whole family. I now know that such reasoning was very erroneous and misguided. My father was too selfish a man to ever think of the general interest. Even when I had the opportunity to bring a relative to join me in Bingué, I still went out of my way to bring my father there. He visited me from February 15th, 2010 to May 31st. We visited the Palace of Grandam, the Parliament of Richelieu, the Eye of Londamou, the embassy of Ebrounia in Gros Carré, and many other parts of Londamou. We visited the towns of Fordia, Luthor, Bardamia and a few villages by car. He was glad to visit the farms of the white binguists farmers which were particularly exotic compared to his own African farms.

At the end of his binguist stay, I gave my father €900 in cash along with new clothes, shoes and other personal effects including a LCD TV with DVD player. He boarded a Glam Airlines flight at Garrick Airport South Terminal. He had worn his big beige coat that I had given him because of the harsh winter he experimented for the first time ever in his seventy-third year. I thought it was no easy task to wear such a heavy clothing item in May for it was such a warm garment. For my father, it was a different story as he felt perfectly comfortable in it. Back in his native country I wanted him to buy a big motorcycle with that money and keep the rest for his personal expenses. Since the Chinese had overfilled the Ebrounien market with those motorised vehicles, prices had dropped considerably. With 300,000 CFA francs, it was easy to buy one. The money he had on him must have been at least 500,000 francs when he changed it into Ebrounian currency.

Chapter 3

Childish day dreams that shaped my destiny

When I was a child, I had a great memory and my brothers entrusted me with certain information that they wanted me to remind them of at a certain moment in time. And I always reminded them of it at the indicated time. I was between three and four years old at the time and I was not yet attending school. It happened that I quickly became aware of my ability to retain information. In fact, I was very early on aware of my intelligence too.

When I was two years old, I was already very eloquent and expressed myself in a sustained language that went well beyond the language acquisition level of the average teenager. Grown-ups found wisdom in me that went far beyond my young age. I remember that in 1972, when my little sister Demba was born, her head was a little deformed because of a football that violently hit the big belly of her mother, Najat, who was returning from the farms close to the early evening. The baby was almost due and the ball hit her on the head of her unborn child. When the adults came to see the baby and to congratulate the mother, I was always the first to tell them that the baby was fine, although its head was somehow deformed by the ball which hit its mother's full-term tummy. They were always surprised that a two-year-old could express himself with such clarity and eloquence.

It was also at that time that the soothsayers, witch doctors and other itinerant marabouts and charlatans that passed through Birgouin prophesied about the clever child I was. At the time, I had the illusion that those people knew how to read in the plans of God as if God himself had no secrets for them. But, today I know full well that they had nothing to do with God. It was by the spirit of the python that they rather prophesied. I was aware that they predicted a bright future for me. They claimed that I would be very well known nationally and that my whole region would be known because of the excellence of my name. According to them I would hold a very prestigious position in the country. Such word of prophecy has always rocked my childhood and my mother in particular liked to run to the marabouts and soothsayers to inquire about what life had in store for me.

I was certainly a child, but she gave me an account of her visits to their shrines and the sacrifices they undoubtedly directed her to carry out. I imagine the little money she had went straight to those fortune tellers but I was unable to stop her. Moreover, my father and my grandmother, Sérida Damsouba, were also aware of all this as various soothsayers and witch doctors also spoke to them confirming what they already knew about my future.

On the other hand, I had those childhood daydreams in which I imagined myself a powerful politician, or someone who held a prestigious public office public and who would advance our region of Bambousso towards development. I wanted to build modern infrastructure in the nineteen villages that made up our region around Tielma, our sub-prefecture. I wanted to modernise agriculture with machinery, modern tractors and combine harvesters, just like the ones in use in the West.

I remember that I found the peasants' manual farm work too arduous and unbearable. And when I put it in parallel with their meagre harvests that could not even feed their families all year round, I came to the conclusion that such thankless harsh labour was an empty enterprise. Indeed, from June to August each year, feeding our family squarely depended on the bags of corn that my uncle Yayous sent down to us from the city of Babiville. I was always flabbergasted by that sad reality because I thought it was inadmissible for corn to come down from the capital city to feed people who were farmers in their village. It is the opposite movement that should be done according to my appreciation of things: take cereals in the village, from the peasants, to send them to the city and not take them from the city dwellers to send them to these peasants in the village.

However, I believe my father was largely responsible for such infamy. Very early on, he had burdened himself with three wives, none of whom was legally married to him. In fact, he had even failed to pay up their bride price that was customary. Then, he was a particularly fertile husband. He produced a dozen children in a short period of time, all of whom were far too young to be productive in the fields. He himself was far from being a champion in farm work.

Hunting in which he excelled could never feed a family of fifteen mouths and that number was soon going to increase to twenty-eight for it would not take him too long in fact to accumulate twenty-four children and to add a fourth wife to his harem!

The worst part of it all was that some evenings, especially from March through June, of each year famine would strike the family. Our mothers would serve us the whole tiny meal of cornmeal called *kabato* and would go to bed with empty stomachs. That was the very heart-breaking scenario I witnessed in my early childhood and I could never fathom it. Our mothers sacrificed themselves for us because their husband had already accumulated three wives by 1975 – at the age of thirty-eight - before adding a fourth in 1980. My father had not yet turned thirty when he embarked on the hopeless adventure of polygamy. All the first three wives were young and they were more or less of equal age and every year, one of them would give birth. Sometimes the first two wives would give birth a few days apart. Sometimes they would produce babies a month apart. Najat and my mother thus engage in a fierce rivalry in my father's home while the youngest, Ndèye, did not really have the heart to stay in such four-person household! In 1976 or 1977, she ran away from her husband, my father, to live with another man in the village at a stone's throw from our compound. The man was much younger than my father who could not face up to him in a proper fist fight. I remember that it was the greatest humiliation a husband had to go through in the history of our village. It went to the point where my classmates laughed at me at school as if I were the cuckolded husband! My only crime was that another man was sleeping with the youngest wife of my dad in broad daylight and that he could do absolutely nothing about it. He was ridiculed for that throughout the entire village of Birgouin for a full year.

His humiliation was thrown in my face as the son of a cuckold man whose youngest wife had been stolen by a love rival. The worst part of it all was that there had been no divorce between my dad and his third wife. Moreover, that young man had not paid the dowry for Ndèye nor did any wedding ceremony of any kind take place to unite them. Such adventure in an improvised home of adultery was a lèse-majesté crime in the context of our traditions which would last about a year and a half. My younger mother - as we, children, referred to her -, got soon bored of that boyfriend, Mindjan. She would soon throw him into oblivion and fall in love with yet another man, a complete stranger who lived in Goudia, the neighbouring sub-prefecture. That was another adventure a little further from home so that my father's humiliation would not be total. He would swallow some grass-snakes for another year until the day when, in 1980, she would return to the village with a rooster and the sum of one thousand CFA francs - which is roughly equivalent to two US dollars -, to apologise to her cuckold husband for her shameful behaviour and ask for his permission to return to his home. Of course, my father was in a real hurry to accept her offer and to wash away the affront to which he had been subjected to for nearly three long years. He was eager to show everyone in the village that he could reconquer his estranged wife.

But during this time, I had a great admiration for Mr. Diomansy, who was an excellent teacher. I had already resolved, around my year four class, to become a teacher like him, to teach and act like him, to pass on my knowledge to the younger generations as he so well did.

Those childish daydreams never left me. I saw teachers as high-level officials then because the clerks of the CIDT, the Ebrounian company for the development of textiles, were civil servants of a much lower level. They were just a notch above the peasants and everyone knew that they had a miserable salary of 80,000 f.cfa at the time.

Also, when I passed the secondary school entrance examination which would take me to high school of Odelta, I met the secondary school teachers there whom I also admired. Immediately, I began to upgrade my ambitions and align them with the destiny of certified English teachers. Mr. Denis, who taught us English in year seven, fascinated me a lot. I wanted to make progress in English and teach that subject. Then Mr. Bamian, who taught us the same subject in year eight, drove the nail in further. I no longer wanted to become a primary school teacher as long as I could become a secondary school teacher.

But in year nine, something happened. Mr. Coulibaly Djakaridja was an excellent French and literature teacher and I was brilliant in his subject. I therefore considered becoming a teacher of literature like him. Then, when I met Mr. Dieng Jules, a Senegalese by birth, who was my literature teacher in year eleven, I was convinced that I had made the right choice. I liked his way of explaining *Sundiata or the Mandinka epic* of Djibril Tamsir Niane. His explanation of Voltaire's *Candide* literally cemented my final choice!

Once in year twelve, Mr. Coulibaly became my literature teacher yet again and I discovered *Germinal* and Émile Zola. The charisma of this particular teacher and his in-depth knowledge have forever drawn me to French literature. Nothing could derail me anymore. After my baccalaureate, I gleefully headed towards that precise sector at the ENS – secondary school teachers' training college - in Babiville.

Once I was there, I discovered any kind of teachers. In fact, they were lecturers and senior lecturers in even more varied subjects: French novel, African novel, oral literature, French theatre, African theatre, African poetry and French poetry, Greek mythology, comparative literature, linguistics, grammar, etc. I was always a lover of novels. I was also a lover of poetry because I was excellent in everything that revolved around the explanation of a text, the essay writing and the commentary. I loved figures of rhetoric which had no secrets for me either. Still, this was different as I had just discovered specialists in various fields related to literature who held doctorates in their specialist field of teaching. I always wanted to become a teacher in the first place but why would I teach in high school when I could become a doctor in literature and lecture in higher education? I decided to further upgrade my ambition yet again. Thus, my resolution was taken. I wanted to become a doctor and become a lecturer, then a senior lecturer before getting to the position of a reader and ending up as a professor.

Already as a child, I constantly used to write on the ground back in my village. Even when we were in the fields and had a little break, I would write words on the ground using my fingers. I wrote words and erased them before rewriting them again and again. I wanted to improve my handwriting. I wanted to calligraph the words as best as I could. It was a never-ending exercise that I did instinctively for many years. In addition to that, I read everything that was printed and on which I could lay my hands. If a sentence appealed to me because of its excellent wording, I would read it again and again to savour its syntax and style.

In the village, we didn't really have a library or bookstore. Besides, I had no money to buy the slightest printed document. But I do remember that within the framework of the single party, everyone was a member of the Democratic Party that ruled the country. As a result, the primary school teachers were all de facto subscribers to Solidarité Hebdo, the party's official newspaper. They would receive their individual copy of it every week in all the most remote hamlets of the country. The party would deduct the cost of that newspaper subscription directly from their salaries every month. I guess they had no choice but to read every publication of that weekly magazine. Sometimes, when they had read those papers and a pile of older issues began to clutter their homes, they would throw them out. I was always going to collect and read them not so much because I was the least bit interested in party politics at that tender age, but to appreciate the writing style of certain journalists whose names and stylistic registers I had come to know. Among them were Bamba Alex Souleymane, Ouattara Hégaud, Jean-Pierre Ayé, K.K. Man Jusu and a few others. I must have been in year five when I started that active reading activity. I was looking for their articles in priority, to read them first. Only then did I read any other article in the newspaper. I didn't mind whether the information was outdated or not : I had found something to read and therefore I had to read it without asking myself any questions. I believe that it was from that age that I nurtured my passion for literature in general and for journalism that I went on to practice in later life.

It is also true that the villagers approached me as early as when I was in year three to ask me to write their letters for their relatives whom the rural exodus had driven to the cities and the forests of the southern part of the country where they could grow coffee or cocoa trees. I always enjoyed writing those letters and I simply calligraphed them to the best of my ability. Some of them asked me to re-read the letter to them. That was to say that I had to translate the letters back into Malinké after having transcribed them into French. When they received the response from the southern areas of the country, they called me back again to go and read their letters. It was a constant exercise because there was always someone who wanted to write a letter or to read one for them. We were very few people around who were able to write or read their letters fluently. In year three, we were the intellectuals of the village!

With hindsight, I understand now that my intellectual ability was very good back then because those students of nowadays simply do not know how to build a sentence that makes complete sense, even for some who are registered in final class of secondary school, year thirteen! I am marking the copies of some of our undergraduate or master's degree students today and I realise the gap that exists between their level and ours when we were in year six. Paradoxically, they are not on the right side of that comparison.

Already in year, we mastered syntactic structures and we knew the basic grammatical rules to avoid making any serious mistakes. We had a good spelling ability too. We read a lot and that definitely helped. Nowadays though, smartphones are at hand. Social networks are everywhere. SMS and emojis are here. No one writes a sentence anymore. We line up acronyms to communicate and go faster. We knowingly massacre the spelling provided that the sound is preserved so that when pupils and students are forced to write in due form, it is a total disaster as they massacre the language and all of its rules. They are simply unable to spell the simplest words in the world. They no longer know any grammar rules. They line up the serious mistakes and are not moved by them. Teachers who mark their papers no longer even dare give them bad grades due to their shortcomings. Despite those colossal blunders, they achieve good grades and progress to higher classes.

It has not always been so. In our time, we did dictation from primary education up until year ten. In year six, we had those difficult dictations taken from the works of Beninese writer, Olympe Bhely-Quenum, which were no easy walks in the park. If put to current postgraduate literature students, 99% of them would have scored naught out of 20. Back in the day, we would lose four marks for a grammatical mistake and two points for a spelling error. Already after five grammatical errors we would be handed out a resounding zero and the teacher would beat us up with his stick which was sometimes a dry wooden ruler or a motorcycle rubber belt. The teacher had the full right to hit us on the fingertips, on our bottoms or in our palms and backs. It was very painful but that was the rule in all the schools around the country. No parent complained back then that their son or daughter had been beaten up for poor school performance. I have always done everything in my power not to suffer those brutal beatings because of bad grades in dictation. The same punishments awaited us though during the rapid calculation exercises whereby we had to work out some tricky calculus in our heads, in a very few seconds, without any calculators. Today I am just sick and tired of seeing young people take calculators to work out what is the change they should give back to a customer that hands over 1,000 francs if they made a purchase of 225 francs!

It is true that we did not have landlines back then let alone mobile phones when we were growing up. There were no text messages at that time either. You had to spell the words and properly calibrate your grammar. I suppose we would pass for purists in the eyes of the current generation. It reminds me of *Things Fall Apart* by Chinua Achebe which I studied with my year eleven. I am pretty sure Okonkwo would agree with me in arguing that the world is definitely collapsing, values are being overturned and standards are crumbling.

Chapter 4

The syncretic beliefs are a hinderance to Africans' blossoming

We were Muslims, or so we were told. I was too, in my own way, since 1977, when I was in year three. My father had sent my brothers and I to Imam Siriki Konaté, whom everyone called Karamoko Siriki, meaning Siriki the teacher. We learned to jabber what we thought was Arabic language, the opening surah of the Quran, the Al Fathya. We were taken on a Friday noon to the village mosque to pray for the first time and we were counted among the Muslims from that day on. Our knowledge of Islam, its doctrine, its prophet and its God was more than skeletal but we were happy to pray and proud to have become Muslims. We couldn't eat warthog meat or smothered meat anymore. We felt grown up and proud to be Muslims!

The Islamic celebrations of Ramadan – *aïd-el-fitr* – and tabaski – *aïd-el-adha* – were happy occasions in the entire village of Birgouin. Everyone in there wore their ceremonial best robes then, preferably white robes. We attended the village mosque in the upper side just a hundred meters before the public primary school of Birgouin. We formed tight rows carefully inspected by Bazoumana Soumahoro who shouted in his sweet voice:

- *Souffouh saffa! Souffouh saffa! Souffah saffa rahamatoumoulahi saffa!* Straighten up the ranks!

We would then squeeze and get closer to one another, shoulder to shoulder, making the effort to draw the straightest possible lines in any rank we found ourselves in.

Just after the nine o'clock prayer, on tabaski feast days, the ram of Karamoko Siriki waited in the courtyard of the mosque and was the first to get the honour of being slaughtered first. When the fat beast's blood would flow all over, the rest of us were allowed to go home where our rams had been waiting for us since the day before. Their life expectancy at that time was much closer to zero. My father, Salman Bamba, would change clothes and dress up in far less sumptuous attire. He would be handed the large kitchen knife specially sharpened for the occasion. He would advance towards the animal slumped on the ground and firmly held by the able-arms of the young people that we were. One of his three wives would come forward to hold one end of his robe (I never understood the spiritual meaning of that act during the sacrifice of *eid-el-ahda*) while he drove the sharp blade into the flesh of the sheep which would bleed profusely. However, we never felt any pity for the poor animal as the blood gushed out like a fountain. Its body would convulse and tremble and we would hold it far too tight to ensure it died quickly. Soon after its passing, it would be fully skinned and dismembered in quarters. It would end up in big pots to enhance the clear sauce and we would then have good food for once a year.

Indeed, meat was generally scarce on our plates on ordinary days, at least in this northern part of the country. I remember that we ate meat when my father was much more able, when he was a very good hunter, a *dozo* as we say back home. Those with education would pretend he was a poacher but to us, in the north, he was rather a *dozo*, someone who commanded respect for his ability to scour the bush in the middle of the night and kill preys that we would discover in his hut the next morning. Over the years, he would bring home countless gazelles, deer, alligators, rodents and other wild animals. On those days too, we would have good food with bushmeat as we called them.

So, we were Muslims, or so we claimed, even though everyone consulted the marabouts, the witch doctors, the soothsayers and other charlatans that lived amongst us as well as those who travelled through the village from neighbouring Mali in search of potential customers. They were consulted for small sums of money or with a new loincloth. They either traced in the sand or threw pebbles, cowries or red or white colas nuts. They jabbered indecipherable words in a language unknown to intelligible humans like us; the language of the genies, the *djinas* as they were called in our language, a bad pronunciation of what the *Quran* calls the *djinns*. After a certain suspense, they would explain our setbacks and harsh living conditions before interpreting the signs traced in the sand, or the position of a sacrificed chicken to tell us if the spirits had accepted or not the sacrifices offered to them. They would invariably indicate further sacrifices to be made in due course to appease the spirits for there is no such thing as a consultation of spirits that is not followed by prescribed sacrifices that must be strictly observed.

The whole village boasted of belonging to the best religion in the world, that of the last revealed prophet, the seal of the prophets that was dispatched at the last minute by Allah to straighten the religion and purify it of all the flaws of Judaism and Christianity. We loved and followed Mohamed Ibn Abdallah as the holiest man to have ever walked on the face of the earth. We were told legends about him during sermons prior to Friday noon prayers as well as during the morning prayers of Eid-ul-Fitr and Eid-el-Adha. None of us could really read Arabic; we simply understood nothing in it whatsoever. At most, everyone tried their best to memorise as many verses of the *Quran* as they could. We tried to pronounce those verses in an alien language that nobody could understand either. It was clear that an Arabic native speaker would not have identified what we jabbered in our prayers and possibly associate it which the Arabic language. But hey, we thought we were praying in Arabic, the language of Allah, the only language that was spoken in Heaven, the only language spoken during the final judgment. At such bet, you might as well try to practice speaking the language here on earth before facing Allah up in Heaven!

Besides, no official ceremony could be held in the village until the Damsouba dignitaries – the traditional leaders of the village – had gathered with great pomp to go and consult the tutelary demons of the village which are called Dongroni and Gbliya. These female genies were supposed to be the real owners of the village and they had to be consulted in every matter regarding the village life. We had to ask for the permission and advice and to hand them offerings and sacrifices, including a goat. We had to make incantations and libations, pour water on the ground and speak on it before immolating the goat. That ritual was rigorously observed before building a school on their territory, a hospital, a water tower, or ... even a mosque! Such blatant religious syncretism was our way of life. It was our vision of the world : to believe in Allah as the only God, the creator of the earth and the heavens while possessing sacred masquerades like the *komo* which was strictly forbidden to women. Moreover, the *komo* had two variants: *kowoulé*, the most dangerous one dubbed Red back, and *dibikoro*, the dismal elder of darkness. I was also initiated to the komo in 1979 like it happened to all male kids in the village who had reached about ten years old. My father had to offer a rooster to the priest of this masquerade, his maternal uncle Soma Bamba. That rooster was sacrificed to the demons behind the masquerade before my brother Yamis and I were allowed to be initiated in the order of the *komo*.

That masquerade came out every year, at least twice a year in fact. It would come out during a sacred dance festival strictly forbidden to women. The dance would last all night long and women were to barricade themselves in their homes until the exhibition of the masquerade was over in the early hours. It would dance and move at surreal speed. It would prophesy about individuals, about the life of the village at large over the coming year or warn villagers of any dangers of drought, bad harvests, etc. It would also indicate sacrifices to be made collectively or individually. All the villagers cheerfully welcomed those prophecies and made the sacrifices with the greatest devotion. In the very same morning, we would go to pray to Allah in the mosque. We surely believed in Allah and we practiced what we knew about Islam but we would keep our fetishes and idols very close to our hearts.

I know now that all of those prophecies derived from the devil. It was through the spirit of the python that the *komo* priest prophesied the future. Moreover, we consulted witch doctors, marabouts, soothsayers and charlatans at the slightest nightmare. As we were Muslims, we had no idea of the interpretation of dreams. In fact, we collectively understood nothing of spiritual matters. We therefore relied upon the interpretation of the marabouts and their acolytes. Thus, they invariably showed us the way of sacrifices to drag us out of trouble. We always had to appease the evil spirits so that they would give us some respite.

When we were little, we travelled through the village trailing the sacrifices offered by random individuals. They were offered almost every week somewhere in the village according to nightmares, indications from the marabouts, the witch doctors, the soothsayers and the charlatans. We would then eat rice dishes cooked with peanut sauce with chicken. It was a treat back then which broke the monotony of the *kabato* dishes, the cornmeal recipe which was usually invariably offered in all the households spread out in the village. We ate *kabato* every lunchtime and every evening. It was becoming unbearably monotonous. We got fed up with it to the point where some of us, who later on ended up getting good jobs in the southern cities, vowed to never eat *kabato* at all for the rest of their lives for they had been left traumatised by decades of uninterrupted consumption of that typical northern Ebrounian meal. When they moved on and made a little more money they would eat rice for the rest of their lives.

The sacrifices or *sarakas*, another mispronunciation of the quranic *saddaqa*, were generally offered hot. The rice and especially the hot sauce sometimes tore our throats out. We still had to eat as much cooked rice as possible when the opportunity arose. Sometimes, there were donuts made from millet flour. Those sweet donuts were called *n'gomis*. Some days, it was *dèguè* that was on offer, which was made from rice flour with milk and sugar. We children were the prime targets for eating the sacrifices offered by adults. We had no idea of the danger that that represented. I know now, forty years on, that it was a way of sacrificing ourselves, a way of transferring the adults' misfortunes and bad luck to us. We have thus sold our future by eating the sacrifices that others have made to ward off their bad luck and negative omen.

During the 1978 Christmas school holiday, my mother, Maya Tamara, took me to Dolan, her home village, to offer a sacrifice to the spirits of Djinako.

That was a river beyond her village in the direction of Goudia, the neighbouring sub-prefecture. We stayed with her uncle, Missamahan Tamara. After the usual civilities, my mother stated the purpose of our visit to Dolan. She wanted to offer a sacrifice of a white rooster and white and red colas nuts to the spirits that lived in those waters so that they would do her good by blessing her eldest son that I was.

According to the beliefs of their family, the Tamaras, there were *djinas* or spirits in those waters, in other words, demons that the religious syncretists considered to be lucky spirits that could bless humans. Although they considered themselves to be observant Muslims, they still brazenly worshipped those spirits which are demons, nothing less. The Tamara family thought they were privileged because those spirits were their own as they revealed themselves precisely to each generation by choosing a male child born from a daughter of the family. Genies would practice matriarchy – which is contrary to the divine law of biblical patriarchy. Well, it was in the name of that matriarchy that they only sponsored a male child born from a daughter of the family and not to the sons of men. According to my mother - I don't know where she honestly got that information from - she was the one that the genies had chosen to honour. However, she would be honoured by and through me, her first son. If I dared to believe her, I was a privileged child that the demons have chosen to bless abundantly. By design, that always translates into a great destiny and a great fortune. I was therefore promised a bright future although it was necessary to offer a sacrifice to the spirits from time to time to renew the alliance between them and me.

It happened that we left for the Djinako river with Missamahan who was to act as the priest that would offer the sacrifice to the spirits on behalf of my mother. My mother carried the white rooster and the cola nuts. When we arrived at the place, which was not very far from the village, I was struck by the tall trees that lined up along both sides of the river banks. It was a true forest in the surrounding savannah vegetation. The trees were tall and colossal in size. Their foliage was lush and green while the trunks were sturdy and firmly planted in the ground which had become damp from the clear water flowing in Djinako's bed. The birds were very numerous in the area, a veritable aviary which uttered so many different cries and sound bites. The insects were also very numerous and they swarmed everywhere. The ecosystem was very fascinating and I imagined that the monkeys in the branches would not be too difficult to spot in that place. Somehow, the place had above all something gloomy and mystical about it. There was such a coolness that cold sweats beaded my spine. I had the confused impression that people were watching us. I mean I believed the spirits were in there and they were listening to us and following our every move. I could feel it, although I could see no other people in there with my physical eyes apart from the three of us.

Soon, Missamahan was to take the white rooster from my mother's hands to brandish it to the spirits and utter a few incantations. He asked them to kindly accept this small present from the hands of his niece, Maya Tamara, on whom their august eyes had fallen to honour her by making her son, Fabien Bamba, a great man in the country. He took the opportunity to introduce me to those spirits so that they could get to know me in flesh and blood. He then put the rooster under his feet, placing its legs and wings well under his left and right feet. He slaughtered the fowl and threw it into the stream of water. The poor beast was struggling big time to try to cling to life as if it were still possible to escape death. Soon after, it expired on its back, with its wings and chest stretched skyward. The priest concluded that this manner of dying showed that the sacrifice had been accepted by the spirits in the waters. He just entered the water to fish out the dead rooster. He also made similar incantations with the white and red cola nuts. He broke each of them into two slices and threw them in the air. The slices of cola nuts fell toss and tails on the firm ground. He concluded that that other sacrifice had also been approved by the spirits.

However, the truth is that I had just been sold out to the demons and evil spirits of the rivers that these syncretic Muslims honoured as gods, thinking they were capable of making people rich and powerful. Apparently, the genies had accepted everything and our trip had been a successful one. Notwithstanding, it turned out that I had to pay a stiff price for that sale of my destiny to the demons. It took me over forty years to understand the spiritual significance of those demonic dealings. They consisted in selling the children to the sirens of the waters, the mermaids which would torment them all their lives. People sold out that way to the water spirits sometimes remained lifelong celibates because of those demonic pacts. Often times, the children sold to the mermaids of the waters became prostitutes; they engaged in extreme debauchery and changed sexual partners like someone changes their shirts. They very often had several children with different sexual partners and their marriages always ended in divorce. They would go through marriage several times during their lives. Alas, all the above shameful narrative programmes that we owe demons of the waters were fully applied to me in my adult life.

It is a delusion indeed to think that demons have gifts in their storehouses for men. They are demons whose purpose is solely to make humans suffer, not to do them good. Moreover, no demon is capable of doing good ever, hence their name as demons. They are no angels but spirits of darkness which cannot offer any light to anyone. Their only business is to make humans suffer; to make a misery of the lives of all those who honour them by worshiping them with sacrifices. As a reward for such worship, they destroy their lives and their descendants' lives over several generations. There is nothing more ungrateful than demons, indeed. They curse those who worship them and then they curse the descendants of their worshippers. Any deal with demons is a fool's deal which they will always repent for!

By the river bank, we made a fire, in the middle of the countryside, on the edge of Djinako, to cook the rooster and eat it on the spot. It was a real communion with the demons which I did not know back then. It was on that day that I was sold to the spirits of the waters without my consent. When you're an eight-year-old kid, you imagine that everything adult parents do on your behalf is necessarily good for you. You give them your full trust, naively. You believe in the legends they tell you and you believe that, because they are adults, they know everything. You believe that they cannot be wrong about anything and that everything they do is surely in your best interest. After all you are their children and they want you to succeed in life more than anything. There is nothing more false than those reasonings of good faith.

For my part, what struck me in the whole scenario was that we ate the chicken roasted on wood fire. It was good food to eat that sacrificed chicken especially since there were only three of us eating it. That is to say that each of us could have eaten more than a quarter of the chicken, which was a lot of meat because when we usually killed a chicken for family, all the cooked fowl to handed over to my father who shared it among all the members of the family after the meal. Imagine a chicken shared between a family of fifteen or sixteen people. But here, on the banks of Djinako, a whole chicken was eaten by the three of us! The colas nuts were eaten by Missamahan and my mother alone. The child that I was did not need them. The unexpected animal protein was more than enough for me. We returned to the village of Dolan shortly after feasting. The same day, my mother and I returned to Birgouin. The mission was well accomplished. I had indeed been sold out to the mermaids of the waters and I was happy to have eaten at the table of the demons! The communion with the demons was so perfect.

That is the unfortunate fate of all Muslims in black Africa : religious syncretism leads them to embrace Islam imported from Saudi Arabia while keeping their hands on the high ends of their traditions and traditional beliefs, which are demonic in essence. They go to the mosque and fast during Ramadan while consulting the marabouts, the diviners and witch doctors to try to read their future, to consult "God", to ward off bad luck and nightmares. They feel that "God" allows them to protect themselves or seek blessings in that way. African Catholics do exactly the same by coming to Catholicism with their polygamy, their mistresses, their alcoholic beverages, their fetishes and their altars. Religious syncretism is the true hinderance to Africans' blossoming.

PART THREE

*BINGUÉ, OR THE MIRAGE OF
INFINITE AFFLUENCE*

Chapter 1

Everyone is affluent in the West, so, let's get the hell out of here!

I was a high school teacher in Becken from October 1996. I was teaching at Belshore Modern High School but I taught at the city's technical high school too as a part-time teacher. I was also an instructor at Campus 2 of the University of Becken in the Department of Modern Letters. Professor Koenan Ackah Lambry was then the director of that campus.

We were teachers with a reduced salary from the very first cohort to suffer such unfortunate fate back in 1991. In fact, we were earning half the salary of our peers that were hired the year before. We were hit hard by way of Decree No. 91-818 of December 11th, 1991 at the instigation of then Prime Minister Ali Watson. However, the peculiar measure was retroactively applied to us although we had graduated from the ENS more than since months before the decree was even signed into law. Moreover, we had been hired by the ministry of national education a couple of months prior to its signature.

Our strikes had done nothing to change it. We had to live with that sword of Damocles hanging over our heads for many years to come. I remember that my first salary, which was paid up in July 1992, was just about 86,000 cfa francs. A complete misery by any measure. At the local treasury office in Dilma, I had been paid such a miserable salary for a secondary school teacher. Back in the seventies, that represented the wages offered to the CIDT clerks who lived in remote villages to council farmers and cotton planters. In front of me, an old Second World War veteran had received his retirement pension of 240,000 francs, three times higher than my salary as a teacher. I have always wondered about that ludicrously unfair salary that Prime Minister Watson unlawfully paid us, retroactively. Asked at a press conference about that legal anomaly, he claimed to be unaware of the non-retroactivity of the law, and he went on to promise to find out about the issue from government lawyers before deciding to exclude us from that exceptional measure. It was all about political rhetoric, of course, and nothing more. The man was not being truthful at that press conference and he never did anything about it as time went by.

Eight years later, we were still struck by that infamous measure. Despite the addition of the accommodation allowance of 40,000 cfa francs per month, and the three successive increases made by President Karl Bédène, respectively of 10,000 cfa francs, then 7,000 cfa francs and 5,000 cfa francs, we were still paid about 158,000 cfa francs per month. Yet, by then, we had eight good years of seniority in the body of public secondary school teachers in Ebrounia. It was just misery all round.

After eight years under such a salary regime, I was fed up. I packed up all my stuff in Becken in July 1999 and vacated my house. I went down to Babiville with my five-month-pregnant wife with the intention of never returning to teach at any school in Becken nor in the country elsewhere for that matter. For me, it was a resignation from my position. I said to myself that, whatever the cost, I would be doing something else at the start of the 1999-2000 school year. I told myself that I would go to Gabbois to try to teach French over there. I had been told that I could earn 700,000 cfa francs per month over there by doing the same work I had been doing in Ebrounia.

But I did not know that fortune had another destination for me. I had not really considered going to Europe. Besides, I wasn't sure if I would get a visa or have the means to buy an expensive long-haul flight ticket to make it that far. While I was finding out about the means of expatriating myself to Gabbois, an elder, Sanga Soumah, asked me my opinion about a possible departure for Bingué. Obviously, I was interested in such an eventuality but how could I afford to pay for such a long trip?

Still, sixty days after that question, I found myself on a Bingué Airlines plane in the direction of Londamou Garrick. Thursday, August 5th, 1999, around midnight, I flew from Borgna airport to Bingué. I arrived there on Friday 6th at around six o'clock. I touched down at the South Terminal of Garrick Airport. There were other illegal travellers like me from several countries. We were escorted in the evening to Haliécourt airport before arriving at the Hotel Lounge in Barlow.

The neighbourhood was chic and we strolled around the hotel so as to not get lost by venturing further afield. We were then looking for a TBC phone booth to call our parents in Africa to let them know that we were in Bingué. I must stress that no direct relative was informed of our intention to go on a short trip, let alone our intention to go so far from our ancestral lands, in a country where we knew no one, and with a language that was almost unknown to us. Admittedly, I already spoke fairly good English since Ebrounia, but speaking with natives of the language was another matter.

From Africa, we imagined that Europe was the Eldorado, that mythical country where people collected a lot of gold and silver in the streets, almost without working. All you had to do was bend down a little low to pick up as many precious stones as you wanted. We thought that the local currency was heavy and that what we would earn from there, even by washing up the dishes in restaurants, would be enough to make us millionaires at home. In any case, this is what we wanted to see in the distorting mirror of quick wealth in Bingué. But it simply turned out to be a myth, nothing more, a mere myth. That myth is probably still quite vivid in the minds of a large majority of Africans applying for Western emigration or choosing to drown or sink in the Mediterranean.

At the time of ignorance, I guess I was asking myself why not go collect my fair share of gold and silver too? After all, I had nothing to lose. The political situation was chaotic in the country. The succession of the old Borgna at the summit of the State was proving perilous with Karl Bédène, who was visibly incompetent and a notoriously corrupt politician. No one had forgotten his penchant for pomp and luxury from the time he was Minister of Economy and Finance of the old days until 1977. It was rumoured that he had fallen out of grace for having celebrated his first seven billion CFA francs of personal wealth. The problem was that such celebration came soon after the vast embezzlement of public funds linked to the construction of sugar production complexes in the north of the country. We always remembered the famous sentence of the old Borgna saying that the country had nothing to do with corrupt executives, even if they were competent. I really wondered what was the definition of the word competent for the old Borgna, and how, according to him, one could be at the same time both competent and corrupt! In short, the gentleman had proclaimed himself president of the Republic of Ebrounia on the evening of December 7th, 1993, using the platform of the 8 p.m. television news reading programme. He had just stepped over the still warm body of the old president.

To hide his incompetence in running the State affairs, he had invented the hollow concept of the twelve building projects of the African Elephant, none of which would ever be carried out in his entire six years at the helm. He would truly prove to be a desperately poor head of State indeed. It was also true that he really did not have much time to concentrate on his projects and plans for the country as he had become insomniac because of his terrible fear of the technocrat Ali Watson, his nemesis who had carved out a solid reputation as a competent and a capable pair of hands that could get the country back to work. His whole programme of government revolved around drafting an electoral code that could indefinitely eliminate his political rival from the presidential races of 1995 and 2000. Quickly though, that obsession turned into dictatorship. He was to issue an international arrest warrant against his rival for *"usurpation of Ebrounian nationality"*. From September 1999, as I foresaw it when I started out as a political analyst, he was to arrest the entire leadership of the PRR – Party for the Rally of Revolutionaries – Ali Watson's party, even though he failed to put his hands on the largest fish who had been enjoying a golden exile in France.

His stubbornness in keeping Professor Hermine Dion Delamare, the secretary general of the party and all the members of the leadership she spearheaded, including Ramadan Gal Congo until Christmas 1999, was to lead, ultimately, to his downfall by coup d'État exactly as I predicted it. I only saw possible two outcomes to the equation that Bédène posed to the country : the lesser one of which would have to be a military coup that would sweep him from power, with the fewest number of casualties possible, and the worst-case scenario, a civil war that would oppose northerners on the one hand to southerners on the other. That option would have immeasurable consequences for the entire nation in my opinion and would unsettle the entire West African region. Needless to say, I was praying and hoping that the first option would take a big thorn out of our way.

It was in that most deleterious political situation that I went to Londamou on Thursday, August 5th, 1999. The following month, Bédène was to arrest and imprison the entire leadership of the PRR. I had been lucky to take shelter at the right time.

Once I arrived here, the immigration services told me that I did not have the right to work during the first six months of my stay in Bingué. However, we were fully covered from accommodation to living expenses, with a postal giro check of €60 per week. We were entitled to free health care, free dental and eye care too, including pharmaceutical glasses. That was a godsend. I took that opportunity to undergo a real eye test at the opticians and get corrective glasses that would eventually be prescribed. That was the first time I had ever worn prescribed glasses in sixteen years that I had been experiencing myopia without being able to afford such convenience.

We did, however, have the right to go to school for free and learn Bingué's language – binguist - and computer science, a tool that I had been desperate to master since I started writing my master's degree dissertation in 1994. It was therefore with joy that I registered at the Golden Gan Farren of Birful, the capital of Gailla where fate had thrown me the day when asylum seekers were dispatched throughout the country. Some left for Glasnord, others for Cherville, Lidantha, Neuchastel, and I left for Birful with my friend Claudia Ballard.

We were housed in Ravière, a popular district in the centre of Birful, a short distance away from the College where we were enrolled. I chose to enrol on a language course at academic level since I already had an intermediate level of acquisition. I was also studying for my first diploma in computer science.

Very quickly, I saved two-thirds of my weekly benefits to buy my first personal computer from a second-hand electrical store. I also bought a large Kenwood hi-fi system which provided great sound. I did not have time for nightclubs or pubs. I did not drink any alcohol nor did I smoke cigarettes either. I was very frugal and I led a very simple and a studious life. I wanted to make the most of that unforeseen student life that was offered to me for free. I did not want to disobey the binguist authorities who had welcomed us so well. I was not seeking to circumvent the laws of the country by trying to work illegally like a few of us did. They would then demand they get paid cash in hand as they had no national insurance number. Some of our brothers did that elsewhere, especially towards Londamou - in the South - where there was a large population of black immigrants. They would impersonate one another, posing as someone who had genuine papers including a work permit and a proper social security number. I was not in a hurry to find a job because I was well aware that I would have plenty of time to do so once the work permit was granted, and I had a better command of the language with IT skills. I have always been an intellectual and I wanted to remain so.

I can say with certainty that not all white folks are rich. I lived long enough in this country of Bingué to understand and see with my own eyes that not all white people are necessarily rich. In fact, many of them are also beggars and homeless people. They would beg for coins in the streets and under the bridges. Some of them asked me to give them money. I saw misery among the white; I saw people who slept outside in the middle of winter, under a blanket. Some of them lived under bridges or in front of stores. Sometimes there would be a dog right next to them, with water or a bottle of liquor.

I visited some houses inhabited by white folks where I came to understand the meaning of the word dirt. Some of them were living in dirt that is out of this world. They have a precise word to designate that kind of filthy place : squalid. The squalid homes are houses that are inhabited but are far too dirty, in extremely poor condition and where an indescribable mess reigns supreme. Everything had a pestilential smell to the point where it took a lot of courage not to hold one's nose once you get in there. The plates were strewn everywhere and had not been cleaned for weeks on end. They were piling up everywhere from the kitchen to the bedrooms and in the living room. They were all dirty; animals would be everywhere, looking hungry, and their waste was visible here and there. Dirty clothes were also strewn everywhere. Furniture would be cluttered with all kinds of dirty or damaged personal effects. The owners of those places were not clean either. You could realise that they had not taken a shower for weeks. They had not brushed their teeth for a long time too although cigarette was always in their hands and mouths, if not cannabis or alcohol. If you looked closely enough, traces of heroin were not far away either. Sometimes, suspicious syringes and equally suspicious spoons were found close by.

I had the misfortune to visit some of those homes, those squalid homes while I was working as a home improvement representative for Belvédère, a company specialising in producing and installing windows, doors, garages and porches to improve homes. Sometimes, when I was offered tea in such houses, it was difficult to press my lips to the rim of the cup in which it was served. It was between September and November 2016. That period of my life left me with a bitter taste. I then understood that definitely not all white people were rich although looking from Africa, the scenery seemed very different : we imagined that all of the West resembled the sumptuous and squeaky-clean dwellings that we saw in films produced in Hollywood. The large luxurious houses with swimming pools, vast green gardens with prolific garages, with big cars parked inside, were for cinema. It was above all the image that Hollywood films and television wanted to project of the Western way of life and that greatly contributes to fuelling illegal African emigration to countries in the northern hemisphere.

I often saw white thieves while I was a supermarket security guard between 2001 and 2002. I was doing that job to fund my doctoral studies. I remember that young Russian student I arrested in the Gasp store in Dalford in the summer of 2001. He had stuffed several pairs denim trousers under his clothes and into a plastic bag. The spoils of his theft were worth over €400. We called the police to have him handcuffed and taken to the police station. Another time, in Birful, there was this young mother who had entered the Ibérard supermarket in Ravière to steal soft drinks and give them to her infant child in the baby stroller. She even hid some more bottles under the pushchair and attempted to exit the store without making payment. I stopped her without qualms. I have witnessed scenes of shameless thefts by white people we thought were all wealthy. I understood that some people were eager to steal peccadillos, simple things that could be bought for peanuts. I just thought no one should do anything to ensure their reputation was tarnished by such silly and petty thefts. Some beautiful and well-dressed up women would come to department stores to steal bras, panties and thongs, etc. They would wear them under their clothes and try to leave the store without making payment. They were also put under arrest despite their breathtaking beauty.

Seen from Africa, that was simply unthinkable : that in Bingué white people could shoplift! However, I saw it with my own eyes. I arrested several thieves – both men and women - when I was working as a security guard in supermarkets. However, at that time, I was only a PhD student. I did not have great financial means but I had enough honesty in me to never consider the slightest theft in any store. In all my life, I have never shoplifted anything, neither in Africa nor in Bingué. It never even crossed my mind. I often went to big stores, especially those that sell electronic equipment to rinse my eyes as they say in Africa. I would study and compare prices charged by various shopping outlets and I would identify the brands and models of electric devices that I wanted to buy once I could afford it. Once those financial means became available, I would return to the store that offered the device of my preferred choice at the best price on the market. In just five minutes, I would collect my purchase and leave the premises with it.

People who live in Africa do not imagine that there can be misery in Bingué. They do not know that some natives of Bingué are tramps who sleep under the stars, if not under bridges. The mirror through which they see Bingué is a distorting one that leads several thousand young Africans to take on the ocean, risking their lives in the hope of making it to Europe! The reality is that some binguist citizens are really rich but those are the few whereas the many others are miserable. Everyone is stressed out. From my experience, there are many more suicides in Bingué than in Africa. In addition, in Bingué there are many more people who need to go see the shrink too – the clinical psychologist, the psychiatrist and the psychotherapist. And of course, we used to earn some money over there, much more money than in Africa for an equal job, but we spent everything in there too. We spent a lot of money in Bingué because it is a real consumer society. They offer everything on credit and everyone buys everything on credit. It goes from homes to mobile phones, from cars to furniture, and to household appliances, etc. The binguist society is one that lives on credit and on borrowing. It is a society that lives excessively to the point where it crumbles under the weight of debt. Everybody owes vast amounts of money to their banks, to mobile phone companies, to internet providers, to department stores, etc. It is a society that lives too fast and burns the candle at both ends, simultaneously.

Chapter 2

The initial attraction suddenly turns to a nightmare

When the work permit was granted to us towards the end of February 2000, I fully intended to further my studies until I passed my first diploma in computer science. Until then, I was doing well in almost all the subjects on that course. If we had to do a ranking like they do in schools in Africa, I would probably be ranked top of my class. I had accumulated good grades – distinctions and merits - in almost all the subjects we studied. But, as soon as the work permit was granted, I was told that I should immediately get into the labour market by registering with the Pôle Emploi to actively seek work and continue to receive unemployment and housing benefits. I was told that to do this, it was forbidden to be enrolled onto a full-time course or training at college. That mean any learning programme of over sixteen hours per week. However, my computer course alone lasted sixteen and a half hours, never mind my four hours of academic English classes that took place in the evening. In total, I already had twenty and a half hours of lessons a week. I was thus ordered to drop out of College with immediate effect and, with a heavy heart, I had to give up on the rest of my computer training in March 2000, having completed two thirds of the course. It was a pity not having the chance to complete the whole course and I was mortified by that injunction, no doubt about it.

My teachers were upset too, including Mrs. Suella Delacroix, who, in the meantime, had become Suella Matthews following her marriage to a colleague of that surname. After all, I was certainly one of the best students on the course. Needless to say that my soul was broken because I had been ordered to drop out of Golden Gan Farren. I was also required to prove it by asking my tutor, Suella Matthews, to deliver me an official letter clearly confirming that I was no longer registered on that IT course. I was to file such a formal letter with Pôle Emploi to prove that I had effectively abandoned my status as a student enrolled on a full-time course, which I did shedding tears.

However, I was not at the end of my troubles just yet. I had to walk through the city looking for work on the computers at Pôle Emploi's offices. I applied for all French teacher jobs advertised on their website. I once had a job interview at a private school for children whose parents were wealthy enough to afford school fees of €19,000 a year. That worked out at twelve million CFA francs per child, in a country where public school is free. I was not offered the job on the pretext that I did not master the curriculum at Bingué schools.

All other applications for intellectual positions I made fell through. I therefore tried to do any other job available because I was under tremendous pressure to find work quickly, else, I was threatened with financial sanction. I was told that my housing and unemployment benefits could be suspended and I dreaded such a prospect. I ended up finding a job as a security guard with a company working for high street department stores across the nation. The salary was above the national minimum wage which was €5.71 per hour at the time as I was getting €8.25 per hour.

Around that very same period, I sought to enrol at university to resume my doctoral studies which were interrupted because of my European trip. I was already in my third year of my doctoral research in Ebrounia under the supervision of Professor Gérald Douga Lézog. It was true that he never read the first draft of my fully written up doctoral thesis that I had deposited on his desk in December 1998. I therefore reformulated my topic of research and presented it to the University from Gailla in Birful and Dr Belma Dior was eager to supervise my work. I am just asked to write to Pr Lézog to obtain his green light to continue that thesis at the University of Gailla. His response was a cold shower that the Professors at the University in Birful could not accept for he had accepted the proposal provided that the thesis remained registered at the University of Ebrounia with the binguist professors acting just like mere tutors. The thesis would have to be defended in Babiville in the presence of those tutors whose travel expenses would be met by the University of Ebrounia. That turned out to be an unacceptable co-direction from the University of Gailla in Birful's perspective. Dr Belma Dior advised me then to seek out Professor Maggie Sirina's availility from the neighbouring University of Glansnann located in Pontiel. This time, I went there without mentioning that the thesis had been registered at the University of Ebrounia. I profoundly changed its title and started all the work research and writing work from scratch. I started to do so on the basis of three years of research to complete the degree.

Nonetheless, another obstacle arose : the tuition fees amounted to €13,000 per year for three years, totalling €42,000. That was more than twenty-five millions in our CFA francs. Where could I find so much money while working as a security guard? How could I reconcile such expense with paying up for my rent and all other living expenses related to transportation, food and clothing? And I still had not mentioned the inevitable western union money transfers to Africa for my parents, my daughter Salma - who was born in December the previous year - and to my wife! I was a modest asylum seeker stuck in a lower end profession which did not require any academic qualification. We had to find a way to cross that financial hurdle and we therefore discussed it with Professor Duncan who found it absurd that they asked more than €42,000 from an asylum seeker to study at the University. At his request, my registration fees are drastically reduced. It was truly a miracle that took place at the time as I was about to throw in the towel once again, having started my research work under the supervision of Professor Maggie Sirina many months before. In the end, all was well that ended well.

Still, to finance my studies, I had to work while carrying out my doctoral research. I had found a job within a security company as I had indicated above. However, it exhausted me because of the many hours spent on the railways. I had to take, at my own expense, a €60 train ticket from Birful to Lidantha for a single night's work. Then, the next day, I had to pay €56 for another ticket to go to Barbaful for another night of work. The following day, I still had to but yet another ticket to go to Survigne, then return to my base in Birful. Sometimes, in the whole month, I would sleep in my bed for only one night and spend the rest of the time on the trains going through Bingué in all directions. I sometimes rested in B&Bs where we sleep and get served breakfast. Rooms in B&B were pre-booked by my employer but all the train tickets were at my expense. They cost me around €1,000 a month or more than 650,000 f.cfa. The downside was that I was only reimbursed for anything exceeding €8 on each ticket. That meant I systematically lost €8 or 5,000 f.cfa outright on each ticket purchased during the month. I could thus lose the equivalent of 150,000 f.cfa on the train tickets purchased each month alone. I would still lose more money from the remainder of my upfront expenditure as my employer would add it to my gross salary, i.e. €650 and they would deduct taxes from that gross income. In the end, out of a monthly expenditure of €900 for my train tickets, I only recouped about €500 and I had to set aside yet another €1,000 for transport the following month. I realised that I had started out that job with savings of €900 in the bank. After two months of work, my account was overdrawn by €80, meaning I had been working to enrich my employer while I got into debt. I ended up resigning from that job without giving notice.

The only advantage to that job was that it allowed me to get to know Bingué well. I criss-crossed the whole country from North to South and from East to West. I knew all the train stations of Berfulia, Williers, Lidantha, Cherville, Sheriffa, Lorgna, Dalford, Swift, Barbados, Barbaful, Nelport, Yelthor, etc. I rubbed shoulders with many binguist people with different cultures and accents in a very short time. I became familiar with those cultures and accents right from my beginnings in the binguist islands in 2000. I was able to tell the difference between accents that binguists people had according to their region of origin.

In Birful, between 1999 and 2002, the black population was an extremely small minority. Sometimes, I would take the bus for a whole week before encountering a single individual from my race. This was why each time we saw one of our fellow human beings, we greeted them with the word "brother" or "sister" as they would do the same with us if they were the first to spot and greet us. That was probably one of the reasons why it was difficult to find black people working illegally in Birful back then. It was simply impossible to miss the colour!

Besides, back then, work was a rare commodity in Gailla in general and in Birful in particular. I realised that once I was forced to leave college and actively seek work. I had gone to meet Suella Matthews in the staff room at the Golden Gan Farren to inform her of the situation. It was much sadder for her because I was one of the best students in her tuition group. With the Afghan Abdulwase, we were the two best students in her class and by far. The least I must say is that finding a decent job in Birful was not really a given thing. There were only a few vacancies for security guards. I had to accept a job by all means to meet the requirements of the Pôle Emploi on the one hand and, on the other hand, to support myself and finance my doctoral studies.

Nothing says our disappointment better when we landed in Bingué on August 6th, 1999 than to learn, after three days, that we had no right to work for six months. We had to get a work permit first. It was an expression that we had never heard of in Africa. We naively thought that we could work as long as we were not lazy. We could not be so emphatically wrong as here, in Bingué, we were told that we must be careful not to work until we secured the work permit which was only issued after six months of actual presence on the territory.

In certain towns and cities where our brothers had been sent, when there was a high concentration of black migrants, they managed to work illegally using fake papers or by usurping the identity of someone else who had the famous sesame. It was a risky tactic because the rules said that anyone caught playing that game would be repatriated to their home country.

I was twenty-nine years old and I had all the time ahead of me. I had enough honesty in me too to wait patiently for my own work permit before looking for a job. Anyway, I thought I was young enough to wait as long as it took. In addition, that time out allowed me to study, to better learn the language of Bingué and also to learn ICT as computers were a tool that I had never used before.

The first winter arrived after three months of stay in Bingué. We could have said that we were more or less prepared for it because we landed in Garrick at the end of the summer. Soon enough the high winds and the rain marking the beginning of autumn were to sweep through the whole country of Bingué. We got used to those rushing winds and incessant pouring rain that is so emblematic of binguist weather. When we were soaked enough like fish, as one should be when one lives on the binguist islands, winter soon arrived. That first winter of our stay beyond the ocean was rigorous. For weeks on end, we saw the whole land of Bingué covered up under a vast immaculate white carpet. The whole country was white like the cotton grown in Birgouin. Sometimes, the depth of this carpet of snow reached twenty centimetres. The walk was difficult and uncertain for that reason. We were sliding as if everyone were walking in a vast ice rink. Some ladies, who were foolish enough to even try to walk in such white mass with high heels, looking just like herons, would collapse awkwardly in the street like Baudelaire's albatross. They needed help to get up most of the time. Some of them would get up from the ground with terrible sprained ankles.

The most striking feature of that initial winter was that temperature was dropping dangerously low. Often times it would sink low to -3° C and the whole body would shiver. The hands would get extremely cold as if they had been drained of blood altogether. You couldn't feel your own fingers anymore. The gloves we bought did not help us much to escape the rigours of that winter of 1999-2000. The roofs of the houses were also covered with a thick layer of snow. The whole district of Jardins Verts was white from top to bottom, like all other districts of Birful for that matter. The inside of houses was beyond cold, a corpse-like coldness that could stiffen a human body in a single night. Fortunately enough though, homes were equipped with heating systems. We were fascinated by those heaters without which life itself would not have been possible in Bingué during winter. Although the artificial heating system gave us headaches, we were forced to put up a good heart against bad luck for headaches were a lesser evil compared to the prospect of certain death from hypothermia.

One of the most surprising things for us who arrived from sub-Saharan Africa - where the sun rises every day at a quarter past six and sets at a quarter past six -, was that in Bingué, even the sun was capricious. In winter, it overstayed in bed and did not wake up until around eight o'clock, thus deceiving workers who had to start their shift at half past seven. Workers had to go to their place of work in the middle of the night, like at four o'clock in the morning in Africa. Similarly, in the evening, Apollo's star hastened to return home and went to bed lazily around three-thirty while workers were far from having finished their day's work. Experimenting such behaviour on the sun's part made us truly speechless when we first arrived in Bingué. At the beginning of August 1999, we saw the sun shining as strongly as possible between seven and eight o'clock. We thought it was daylight and we would go to offices and stores for administrative procedures or for shopping. They would simply be found hermetically locked. We later understood that people in Bingué did not take into account the vagaries of the sun but the time on the clock. They chose the good old Chronos over his grandson Apollo. Once time was up for a day's shift, officials and shop clerks would go home. Their work usually ended around five o'clock whether it was night or day, it didn't matter to them. They would go home until the next day.

On the other hand, the winter solstice was even more surprising for us because around half past three, the country would be plunged into absolute darkness. It was like being in Africa at eight o'clock. Only electricity then allowed us to see clearly and the administrations and businesses continued to operate in the middle of the night as work was not yet finished and would hardly be until five o'clock.

Those phenomena of the capricious nature disconcerted us to the highest point as we were not prepared for such dramatic changes one bit. Indeed, we were all the more confused each time the season changed. Amazingly enough, that was not so much the end of our surprise though as there was another phenomenon, a cultural one this time, which astonished us to the highest degree. No one greeted the other person here in Bingué. Potential customers would walk into stores, look shop assistants straight in the eye and walk pass them without greeting them. They would go on to admire goods on display and would sometimes come back to the same shop assistants at the tills to make payment. It was as if they had forgotten the fact that they did walk pass them without greeting any of them when they entered the store. We definitely thought everyone was rude here in Bingué. Otherwise, how could we explain that one found a human being in their workplace without having the civility to greet them and wish them a good day? Even in the workplace, colleagues did not greet each other systematically either as it was appropriate to do so back home in Africa. Similarly, they would neither say goodbye to each other at the end of their shift. Definitely, all the rude people had met in Bingué, we thought! We agreed they lived side by side instead of living together as good neighbours.

We were shocked further to see that everyone was walking around with their lunchbox. When time came for lunch break, everyone would sit in a corner and eat alone, without inviting anyone else to share their meal. And they continued to chat with their friends and colleagues while eating. However, no one thought it was a decent and a honourable thing to invite their neighbour to share their meal. We thought that, definitely, here in Bingué, everyone was mean and selfish. How could they eat in front of their neighbour without sharing their food with them? We thought it would be nice for someone to sacrifice to the old human tradition which dictates that one shares their meal with one's neighbour who had none. Did not the wise Seydou Badjan Kouyaté write in *Sous l'Orage* that cooked rice belongs to everyone?

Something even more surprising was still in store for us : when we visited comrades, taking leave of them, they never saw us off. At most they would leave us at the door and close it behind us. We would then walk home alone. However, in our culture conviviality required that we accompanied halfway home the one who visited us. We usually walked halfway with them before taking leave to head back home. In this way, everyone got home almost at the same time. Worse still, a friend would take you out to eat and, after the meal, would expect you to split the bill with them! Why invite someone to dinner if you couldn't afford to pay for dinner or lunch for both? What is the meaning of such an "invitation"? Truly, binguists had weird ways of living. It seemed to us that Bingué had washed its citizens of their humanity. That was why we were pleased to have a very African tradition made of humanism, mutual respect, solidarity, caring and sharing. We were therefore determined to preserve that cultural heritage.

Chapter 3

To succeed in Bingué, you have to study at its local universities

Until then, all the Ebrounian diplomas that I presented everywhere to look for work were not worth a penny. I was told that my Ebrounian baccalaureate was worth nothing at all. The CAP/CEG of the ENS, which gave me the right to be a French teacher in general education colleges in Ebrounia was absolutely worthless too. Never minding those hard facts, I showed them my degree from the National University of Ebrounia. Certainly, that university degree would mean something to them. But nay! Even when I presented my master's degree and my DEA - Diplôme d'Études Approfondies - from the same institution, I was dismissed as someone who had never graduated from a higher education institution. I understood one thing then : to achieve things in the binguist society, or in the Western society at large, it is absolutely necessary to study at local European universities.

There is indeed a sovereign contempt for diplomas and degrees obtained overseas as they say, meaning in poor countries. They just do not count at all. You must obtain an equivalence of your diplomas from your native country and apply to complete your studies in a binguist university. I therefore wrote to KRINA, the body that handles such matters in Cheldam for €35.

So, I took the plunge and I was much surprised when the official decision fell : my BEPC from Ebrounia was valued below the binguist BEPC. My baccalaureate was equivalent to the binguist certificate of general school education with the exception of English and science. My CAP/CEG as a secondary school teacher was deemed to be the equivalent of the binguist secondary education certificate too. My bachelor degree and my master degree were worth next to nothing. It was my degree of advanced studies which was accepted to be the equivalent of the binguist bachelor degree with honours. I was shocked and stunned. Was there really so huge a difference in educational quality between Bingué and Ébrounia?

I still accepted everything that could be offered to me as a parchment from KRINA, just to allow me to enrol at a binguist university in order to complete my PhD. It was therefore with great anticipation that I enrolled at Glansnann University in Pontiel around May 2000 to do a PhD in French novels of the 19th Century. I chose to stay in line with my master's dissertation in 1995 at the University of Ebrounia in Babiville which dealt with *La Curée* by Émile Zola and my DEA in 1996 on the *Rougon-Macquart*.

This time, I had a hell of a chance because the libraries of the University of Gailla in Birful and of the University of Carambert were huge and very well supplied. I found there the edition of the *Rougon-Macquart* in five volumes under the direction of Professor Emeritus Henri Mitterand. I also found there the *Dictionnaire de la Langue Française* by Maximilien

Émile Littré in its original edition of the years 1863 to 1872. There are, especially in Carambert, all kinds of publications on Zola and naturalism, the doctoral theses by some famous names, various critical studies, the proceedings of colloquia on the author and on naturalism, etc. I documented myself constantly and almost for free. I often left Birful for Carambert to spend the whole day there photocopying all the research material that interested me before going to digest them at home.

In the meantime, I moved to Fordia in September 2002, just a few kilometres away from Carambert. It was therefore much easier to commute between those two south-eastern towns of Bingué. I read a lot and took precise notes on the aspects that were likely to be quoted in my written work.

When I submitted a draft of my thesis on the table of my supervisor, Professor Maggie Sirina, she would summon me up to show me her report two weeks later, with precise notes, word processed and printed out. I would sit opposite her desk and listen to her religiously. We would go through my thesis from page to page and I would leave her office with the printout of her remarks. I would work on it again before reporting back to her in the following two weeks. That was how we completed the work after three years and the defence took place on August 21st, 2003.

The jury was chaired by Professor Rachou Keller, who was the external examiner and also the head of the Department of Foreign Languages at the University of Lorgna. It also included Dr Belma Dior from the University of Gailla in Birful, who acted as an internal examiner. I remember that the defence had nothing to do with what I was used to seeing in Ebrounia where it is a public event attended by the candidate's parents and friends as well as a crowd of complete strangers.

There were the two examiners and myself, the candidate, when I defended my thesis. Everything happened behind closed doors. The questions put to me were relevant in the sense that the examiners were seeking to better understand what the candidate meant, or for him to elaborate more on some aspects. Questions were also asked about the content of certain bibliographic sources but the tendency was not to show the candidate that he knew nothing and that he would benefit from listening better to the masters of the craft. The candidate was therefore not ''defending'' his research work against people who wanted to destroy it. The defence lasted between three quarters of an hour and an hour maximum. They delivered my result : thesis admitted! However, there was no special *''mention''* that was attributed at that level contrary to what I was used to seeing in my country of origin where the mentions *"Honourable", "Very honourable"* do exist, with or without *"Congratulations of the jury"*. I was told that for Anglo-Saxons, all PhDs were equal and that they are not followed by any such mentions. Moreover, the candidate could be declared to have passed, or admitted subject to making some changes that they would have to make to their research work in three months or up to a year, or that they were outright adjourned. In such case, they would benefit from an extension of one year, or six months, to profoundly overhaul they work in a certain direction. If they were ready for the second time, they would defend their thesis once again.

The graduation ceremony took place at the University of Glansnann on December 16, 2003. I had meanwhile bought my second car, a seven-year-old Hyundai Lantra with a particularly low mileage. The car was beautiful and in top mechanical and electrical shape. I was driving to Birful from Fordia that morning in the car and two good friends of mine offered to support me on the day. They were the only family I had to show me such support me at graduation. They were the Cameroonian Stephen Bassi and the Ebrounian Oumar Sacko. We left Fordia at around four in the morning, relying solely on a Bingué map. TomTom and other GPS navigators were not yet popular. We first took the AA421 national road before arriving at the AM1 south motorway. We descended towards Londamou down below before turning right to take the Londamouenne ring road called AM25. We then turned to drive along AM4 motorway which connects Bingué to Gailla from Londamou. We drove about four hours and crossed over the gigantic and magnificent Sovereign Bridge of Gailla, more than five thousand yards long. At the time, it was just known as Pont Croissant because it overlooked the huge Croissant River. It was a kind of natural border between Bingué and Gailla. It is a very impressive structure for anyone crossing it for the first time. My African friends were naturally amazed to cross it and I remember that I was too, on Monday August 9th,

1999 when I crossed it for the very first time in my life.

Back then, we were driven in a mini bus by a Hindu driver. On that initial trip, we left Londamou for Birful where fate had wanted to send us, my friend Claudia and I plus two Ecuadorians, Luis Enrique Obando Montenegro and Cecilia Gutierrez. We were then travelling under the orders of the immigration services and under the supervision of Sorali, a Somali lady working for the Refugee Council. The two South Americans did not understand a single word of Bingué's language. Claudia did not understand much more than the usual greetings either. Fate therefore wanted me to serve as a natural - and free - translator for her and for them. So, I translated from binguist to Spanish and from Spanish to binguist for those two South Americans but also from binguist to French and vice versa for Claudia. That was to be the case for the entire months of August and September 1999.

When we had to go to the hospital for extensive medical examinations, including chest X-rays and tuberculosis tests, I had to translate for them all the doctors' questions and their answers to the doctors. When it came to enrolling at Golden Gan Farren, I also translated their entire interview with the teachers. My Spanish, which was beginning to slumber and die out inside of me, was therefore rapidly brought back to life.

Anyway, that was a long time ago. Already four and a half years had passed since those things had happened. Today, I am due to receive my PhD in

French literature of the 19th Century. I am dressed up in a grey suit and I will soon be wearing the blue and yellow gown, the ceremonial dress for solemn graduation ceremonies at my University. I had already paid up front the cost of renting my gown and my doctor's hat before coming here, around €150. The hat way round for doctors while it was diamond shaped for bachelor's and master's graduates.

It was a lovely ceremony and I received my degree from the hands of the Chancellor of the University at around eleven o'clock. Before that, the photo-taking ceremony has already taken place at around nine-thirty with a white and hard fake parchment. I did not know whether it was made of moulded cardboard or plastic, but in the photo it looked like a real diploma rolled up and tied up with a bright red cordon.

The day was going well and everything was good-natured. We returned to Fordia at around four-thirty the same evening. It was still eight hours round trip on the motorway. I was particularly proud of my friends who were kind enough to travel with me to support me so far from their base. They had to make the sacrifice of taking time off from their respective jobs that day in order to make themselves available for my big day.

I was also happy on another level, probably an illusory one, but I did not know it at the time. I told myself that finally, I was at the end of my troubles because employers would have no choice but to sit back and respect my PhD awarded by a binguist University. I was now Doctor Bamba after all, and I would be able to apply for a lecturership in any University in Bingué. I already dreamt of joining a Department of French Studies starting from 2003-2004 academic year. I was sure of getting a job right from the very first applications I would make. My head was filled with scientific projects and wild academic dreams.

The following days, I was in heaven. I called my wife, Kyria, who was still living in Babiville to break the news of my academic achievements to her. I also called my parents and extended family to share the good news with them too. They all rejoiced with me. Like me, they too were in dreamland. They believed that I would become a great man in the country of Bingué. As it was during the summer holiday that I had defended my thesis, I thought that as soon as the following academic year, in September 2003, I would find a job as a lecturer in a binguist University. When that did not happen, I was not unduly alarmed. I imagined that after the graduation ceremony the following December, I would have more credibility with employers. I was convinced that with my degree physically available, I would have made a difference for I could produce it and employers would snap up my services like one buys freshly baked bread. Again, I was living in illusion but I did not know it just yet. However, I should soon find out at my expense that there was no reason so to be so overly optimistic!

It is just crazy the tricks life can play on you sometimes. You are young, you are well trained and you would like to think you are competent and capable of accomplishing anything and, suddenly, no one lets you set foot in the stirrup. As a result, the years pass by and your hair begins to turn to grey and then to white. Your ambitions then begin to wither over the years. You also bend under the weight of the lost years as you agonise under the unfulfilled dreams and promises. Your wildest dreams turn to nightmares. The level of self-confidence begins to drop sharply like shares on the Londamou stock exchange on a day of financial massacre. There is nothing whose market value plummets faster than a degree which does not immediately allow you to get on the labour market. A used Ford Fiesta, for the same number of years, would sell much better than such University degree. I did not know that my PhD would only be sold on the market after some nineteen long years of disappointment.

Chapter 4

Degrees are not the parchment that open the right doors when you are of dark complexion and have a name that is exotic, to say the least.

Soon enough, I would realise the sad and obvious fact : when you have a black African sounding name, you have much less chance of being recruited into higher education in Bingué – or in any other high-end position. In any case, candidates whose surname is typically binguist have a much better chance of being among the shortlisted candidates whom would be offered a job interview.

From the very first job applications, I realised that obviousness. At first, I told myself that it was bad luck that I was not selected each time I was interested in a position advertised on the academic employment website. But, what made me tick was that I applied for a lecturer job in Francophone Studies at the University of St Bernard. It was a renowned old University, an august institution indeed, the University where the dolphin, the future monarch, studied and where he met the future princess Dalila Ricœur, the future queen. I was not selected and the institution did not even give me a sign to acknowledge that it had received my application for employment as it was customary. Three months later, the same position was still advertised on the website for a candidate specialising in French literature of the 19th

Century. In addition, the right candidate would have to be near-native fluent in French.

I fulfilled all the criteria and beyond but, somehow, I had not been selected the first time. Never minding that, I applied for the job once again. I was not on the shortlist either for the second time around. I was not given any feedback to let me know if my application had been received at least as was customary in such circumstances. No one was recruited to the position that time either, like the first time three months before. Three months later, the same job was advertised again on the website. I finally understood the thing clearly : they definitely needed a candidate to fill that position but they did not need me, Dr Fabien Bamba.

My name certainly sounded far too African and too black for such a beautiful and prestigious institution that trains princes and princesses that would inherit the crown in Bingué. I therefore understood that degrees were not the parchment to open the right doors when you are dark-skinned and have a name that is exotic - to say the least - in a so white country and with ancestral and thousand years' old traditions.

That third time, I did not even waste my time applying for the job at all. Examples like that were legion where I applied for a job as a lecturer in French Studies without the University contacting me to tell me that my application had been received. In principle, they are required by law to show such courtesy, and even to notify candidates who were not shortlisted. Regardless, they just ignored me time and again. In all, I applied more than eighty times for as many positions in binguist Universities with the same outcome : total silence. Only once did someone write back to me to tell me that my application had been received and that I would be notified if I was on the short list of potentially suitable candidates for filling the position. Then nothing. After my eightieth attempt, I gave up completely on my desire to hold a lecturership position in binguist higher education institutions.

I decided to stay in secondary education as a supply teacher. I would replace any teacher that was is on leave from their post for a day, half a day or longer. The pay was certainly not bad, between €140 and €150 per day or half that amount for the half day teaching. However, it was really not for such amount of money, nor for this work, that I decided to do a doctorate to go and teach simple things like *"Hello, my name is John and I am twelve years old. My father's name is Adam and my mother's name is Julie''*. I know I am worth far more than such B-A-BA.

I soon began considering returning to the country of origin to try an academic adventure over there and to potentially rise to the rank of professor before I retire. I had a problem though; a problem that has haunted my life for almost twenty years. I was a civil servant in my country of birth and I had given up my position as a secondary school teacher to fly out to Bingué without administrative authorisation. It was a case of abandonment of position after eight years of service when I had signed up a ten-year commitment to the State when I left the training college, ENS, the institution which trained us as secondary school teachers.

That was going to be a lingering obstacle to fulfilling my ambitions. In 2008, after five years of dithering in Bingué, I ended up submitting a job application hoping to be recruited in the public universities of my country of origin. The Ministry of Public Service held by Hibou Dormeur of the PFI at that time vetoed my appointment although the Ministry of Higher Education and Scientific Research held by Baroudeur Charlie and that of the Economy and Finance held by Claude Lenoir were both in favour of my appointment. The veto of the representatives of Hibou Dormeur prevails because it was based on the argument that I was a former civil servant who had given up his job and vanished. With a higher degree, he wanted to return home to occupy a higher position without going through the process of the reinstatement procedure and possibly through the disciplinary council that dealt with such cases.

Even when I tried to go back in 2011, after the political regime had changed in Babiville and Ali Watson was in charge, that question of prior reinstatement in the Civil Service once again dashed my hopes. I ended up deciding to stay in Bingué to try to earn as much money as possible. Besides, my family, whom I brought from Africa on June 14th, 2005, was not very enthusiastic to see me go back to settle in Africa while they stayed behind in Bingué. So, I gave myself a host of reasons not to force a return to my native country. My children Joshua and Salma had already become binguist citizens just like their father. Their mother, Kyria was about to become one a citizen too from 2010. I told myself that I had everything here to earn a living and acquire everything I wanted. I already had a job and I could have projects and, with some effort, I could implement them.

In addition to all the above, I remember that it was recommended to me to come and settle in Ebrounia for at least four good months, to begin a procedure of reintegration within the Public Service. I would also have to wait for the result of such procedure and respond immediately to a possible summons from the Civil Service Disciplinary Board to go and justify the abandonment of my position, which had gone on for at least ten years. I imagined, wrongly, that those four months were a wasted too long time in my life, four months of doing nothing, earning nothing. And I had to live in a country that was no longer quite mine, without any financial support of any kind. Moreover, in the event of reinstatement, I would be paid approximately 400,000 f.cfa per month (2008 salary), which represented a drastic salary drop of more than three quarters in my case.

It was a reasoning that I would have to regret and repent for a long time because those who were recruited precisely in 2008 – five years after my PhD – as lecturers in the country's public Universities became professors years ago. With my recruitment in 2022, I have to call them *"masters"*. In life, everything is all about timing, indeed. If you miss certain decisive turning points in your life, you are off to a very bad start. Some current professors were undergraduate or postgraduate students in 2003 when I became a doctor. I must now pay the consequences of my bad choices made in the past and redeem the time. It is all about time and informed choices and decisions.

Anyway, I remained a supply teacher in binguist high schools and colleges for nineteen years. That career started in September 2002 in Fordia where I worked for ADA Ltd and for Delta Education Ltd. Later on, Damien Sherman left ADA and founded Golden Education Ltd with Sharon who left Delta Education Ltd. I travelled extensively in the South-East of the country and I knew all the schools in the area, or almost. I taught in Luthor, Belzard, Ayfield, Bardamia, Peterla, Hundia, Carambert, St. Bernard, Buckfiel, Luthor, Wellingan, Wamarth, St. Buckens, Hemellia, Berkins, Mansul, Bigging, Barfondia, Selbourg, Letchang, Hittingon, Stevrad, Boredom, Hatfarland, Herbourg, in Dalmina, etc.

I have undoubtedly taught more than ten thousand binguist students aged eleven to nineteen over a period of nineteen years. I have always been happy to find former students working in banks who recognised me as their former teacher in such and such school. It was enough hard to remember their faces because I had often done a single day work in some schools or only an hour lesson with some of them and I moved on. Besides, I had never really been a physiognomist, but it felt good to have several of those former students, as well in Ebrounia as in Bingué, rising to all ranks of social and professional life. Some became bankers, lawyers, doctors, teachers, academics, etc.

That is, I believe, the only real satisfaction of the teaching profession. The true salary of our endeavour is there and not elsewhere.

I have known several young intellectuals who migrated to Bingué but who had great difficulty finding work in their area of expertise. Some engineers had thus become salesmen, warehouse operatives, security guards, etc. The situation of accountants was not much better. Those who clung to their area of qualification were forced to settle for freelancing or working for temp agencies. They were day labourers who were willingly tossed from one place of work to another, with gaps in their employment history lasting sometimes up to six months or more.

It all begins with the under-rating of graduate migrants. When they had degrees in their home countries, they were told it was worth a far inferior binguist degree. They went so far as to tell them that they were not qualified. An African qualified teacher who is a migrant in Bingué becomes an unqualified teacher and they must resume their higher education there if they ever want to freely pursue their teaching career in Bingué. It is not even so straightforward though as they must do a binguist teaching qualification, the CAPES. That requires them to retake Bingué's general secondary school certificate with fairly good honours in mathematics, science and English even if they want to teach German, Spanish or PE! The BEPC or the baccalaureate awarded in Africa are worth nothing in Bingué. If the migrant teacher has an advanced university qualification like the PhD, there is no exception to that rule. Even if they concede that they have the required knowledge in mathematics or in science, it is argued that their English is below the required standard. If the migrant teacher is stubborn enough and still wants to teach in the long run in Bingué, they must agree to resit the BEPC in those three fundamental subjects. If their results are deemed good, then they can go on to pursue a CAPES at University over two years. Only then can they be called a qualified teacher.

That being said, the fundamental value that I have found in the binguist education system is that it has zero tolerance for interpersonal relationships between teachers and students. There is no exception to that rule. As a result, there are very few female students who become pregnant during the school year. It is not that teachers do not absolutely have any romantic relationships with their students whatsoever, because there are still some few who dare do so. But the few cases that arise happen only in absolute secrecy. Once suspicion arises, the teacher is suspended immediately. An investigation starts right away and if there was any truth to the allegation, then the teacher is systematically removed from the profession for life. He or she is forced to sign the sex offenders register for life if the student was a minor, which drastically reduces their chances of finding a new job away from the education industry. No one likes working with a known paedophile. Paradoxically, the most frequent cases involve female teachers who have a culpable relationship with underage male students. In any case, the penalty is the same for all the culprits and it is merciless. I thought that if such a measure were introduced in Africa, we would make great progress in that area and pregnancies in schools would be very rare indeed.

In Bingué, they take this matter so seriously that teachers are not allowed to give students their mobile phone numbers, or ask for theirs. Likewise, they are not allowed to be friends with their students on social media for fear that they might make a move on them and see each other outside of school for impure reasons.

I remember meeting a young fella in Kempsis, near Fordia, a Zimbabwean teacher who was well liked by his middle school students. He was very popular and very funny, I reckon. All the students liked him as he used to joke with them during break and lunch times. He was a gifted comedian capable of entertaining a large room with some terrific one man show performance. Sadly, he ruined his career in 2004 when he gave his mobile number to a white female year eight student. The girl's parents discovered that he was communicating with their daughter and reported him to the headteacher. The facts were proven even though nothing cynical had happened between them. However, he was unceremoniously dismissed without further warning. It was ruled that he potentially had a sexual interest in that child.

That law is so strict that a teacher is not even allowed to touch the arm or any part of a student's skin. They just do not touch them, both boys or girls because there are also many people who may have an exclusive interest in people who are of the same sex as themselves. That is why a teacher cannot justify his innocence by claiming that the student they touched is of the same sex as themselves, therefore they definitely had no sexual interest in them.

On the other hand, the weakness of the system lies in the way of managing the cases of slanderous denunciations which are unfortunately numerous and exceed the real cases. I remember that white deputy headteacher who had nearly twenty-eight years' experience as a teacher. Out of the blue he had been maliciously accused of having sexually harassed a young girl in year nine. It was a tissue of lies because the young girl found him too strict and had determined to ruin her career. He was suspended immediately and the investigation lasted two long years. Meanwhile, he had nothing else to live on. He was technically unemployed, without a salary, without dignity. In the end, he was completely cleared of all wrongdoing and the girl confessed her malicious motives for revenge. The man was rehabilitated but his career and reputation were already ruined. How does one rebuild their life after suffering such public torture and humiliation?

The man did not understand why his irreproachable career as a teacher and a respected deputy headteacher for nearly thirty years had not weighed a penny in his favour. He wondered why a mythomaniac dreamer like that student was allowed to ruin the life and career of a professional like him in the blink of an eye, without anyone listening to him or giving him the benefit of the doubt.

I know something about that now because my own daughter Alesha put me through almost a similar situation for two years too. It is true that she never claimed that I had sexually abused her. At most, she claimed that I had beaten her up in such and such way, kicking her in the stomach with my shoes on my feet, or that I had beaten her up with my belts. The consequences were just as dramatic as for the deputy headteacher mentioned above. Like him, I was suspended from my duties the day after the accusations. As with the deputy headteacher, the investigation lasted two years. As for the deputy headteacher, my life had stopped during those two years. Like this deputy headteacher, my professional career of twenty-six years was not worth a nail. Like the deputy headteacher, I was considered *a priori* as a criminal and not presumed innocent. I was presumed guilty until it was established that I was innocent after all.

You never recover from those things. You relearn to live with them, to take a step forward at a time, then another, if possible. Human dignity is a very perishable commodity indeed and it is not uncommon for it to suddenly evaporate, with a single malicious accusation. Building a reputation can take decades of hard work, or even an entire career of honesty and selflessness. However, seeing it shatter is a matter of a few minutes. And the worst thing is that it is completely out of the victim's control since the accuser's voice comes from the outside. It is the voice of the other, of the accuser, who is a third person, with their own ambitions and motivations. That person totally escapes your control but you can never escape them. It is like the grim reaper that is watching you, and which will certainly end up claiming your skin!

PART FOUR

WHEN WE WERE HAPPY IN OUR COUNTRY OF BIRTH

Chapter 1

When you excel in training and educating young people in your own country, you contribute effectively to its development.

I taught for eight years in Ebrounia before leaving the country in 1999. When I entered the Civil Service, I was barely twenty-one and a half years old. I was absolutely beardless, without a moustache, a real baby-faced teacher as they would say in Bingué. I was not strongly built either and I barely weighed fifty-eight kilos. I was looking no older than some of my students. Some of them were indeed twenty-two years old while their teacher was one year younger. For them, calling me sir and submitting to my authority was a real challenge.

I began my career in October 1991 as a high school teacher at the Municipal College of Garbour, a provincial town in the country. It was in my presence that Lucien Gueulard was elected in 1992 as a Member of Parliament for the Garbour constituency. At the time, it was a town of some two or three thousand people, a third of whom were made up of students from the municipal college and the private college Angelbert Labelle. Coming from Dilma, on the left, there was the dusty main road that crossed the town to the sub-prefecture offices. I lived just on the left-hand side of that main boulevard, almost at the end of it, a few hundred meters away from the office of the sub-prefect. It was a four-room Sicogi house with a fairly large garden. It was built in the 1970s or so I was told. The rent cost 20,000 f.cfa per month, not much to tell the truth. The architecture was very simple : just three bedrooms and a living room, a single bathroom inside without a toilet because there was no running water in Garbour at the time. In the backyard, a small house that served as an old-fashioned toilet : a small hole in a concrete slab above a septic tank. You had to be dexterous in aiming for that narrow hole if you did not want to do an inconvenient clean-up afterwards. The house was still fine and it was not particularly hot inside.

That was where I lived for three years and where I planned my first French lessons for the year sevens, eights, nines, tens and eleven. Luckily, we still had electricity even though we lacked a post office, a bank, ATMs, a hospital or a pharmacy.

Nonetheless, water was Garbour's most crucial problem. We had to buy unclean and unsafe water carried in tanks by Malians who sold twenty-litre cans at exorbitant prices. They were called *djitiguis*, which translates as owners of the water in the Malinké language. They transported the cans of water in their carts called *wottros* and a barrel of two hundred litres cost 400 francs to fill. In the month, it was a fortune, more than twelve thousand francs to poison oneself with undrinkable water. Every two or three months, it would make me really sick. I often had diarrhoea that made me feel like I was going to die. I had to run to the pharmacist to get prescription drugs against bacteria and various parasites every month to stay alive. It was a real hassle to drink that water and cook with it. If our life was in danger in Garbour between 1991 and 1995, it was because of that contaminated water. It was the main reason why I asked to be transferred to Dilma Modern High School in October 1995.

The good thing though was that I got my first taste of teaching there and gained valuable teaching experience in the process. After two years of practice in the teaching profession, I no longer needed to plan my lessons. With a piece of white chalk, I could go on and deliver an excellent French lesson because I had all the lessons structured in my head. I just had to know the last line of the previous lesson to carry on with the next lesson. Little by little, my students had noticed that pedagogical excellence, although they complained that I was too strict in granted high marks. It is true that I was very demanding in the area of evaluation and assessment. I was a perfectionist who refused to accept grammar mistakes and even spelling mistakes, including missing or extra accents.

It was also in Garbour that I took became an unfaithful lover. I was a young teacher between twenty-one and twenty-five at the time. I was single and there were many young ladies in town or passing through that sub-prefecture. That was where my fellow civil servants and I started having an unbridled and a shameful love life. I ended up becoming an unfaithful partner to any girlfriend who hooked up with me. Of all of them though, Dalia Amar is the one who caught my heart. She just stoop up from the crowd for I dearly and truly loved her.

I met her in 1993-94 when I was living in Garbour. She was born in the town and was pursuing her Physics studies at University in the capital city. I was a teacher but also a studying for higher qualifications. I was awarded the bachelor degree in French in 1992 during my first year as a teacher in that small town. In 1993, I had completed my C2 - the first part of the master's degree and in March 1995, I had defended my master's degree dissertation before immediately registering for the advanced degree known as the DEA, equivalent to Mphil.

When I met Dalia, I found her very charming, not particularly pretty in the sense of Miss Universe, but with such harmony of the body, and such sweetness that she was the perfect woman. She was in her third year of Physics at the University of Ebrounia but she was born in that town where her parents lived. Admittedly, her father had passed away for a long time. She did have her mother, her stepfather and her daughter, Sylvia, born of a previous relationship in 1986. Sylvia was a year one student and her mother frequently came over to see her and spend time with the family. Her grandmother lived just across the street from my place and I don't know how on earth I had not met her sooner.

In 1993, around the beginning of the school year, I had met her. We introduced ourselves to each other and soon I was to visit her at her grandmother's house and she was to visit me at mine. We spent hours talking, without necessarily talking about a romantic relationship but it was clear that that was what we both wanted. She was intelligent like no other. Dalia did not need me to use words to read my mind nor did I need to wait for her to articulate sentences to understand her thinking. It was such a harmony of thought, a real telepathy to the point where I concluded that she was my soul mate. Besides, before I declared my love to her in words, I had that premonitory dream according to which she was lying on my chest, listening to my heartbeat, while we were madly in love with each other.

One evening as we were talking in my bedroom, I related that dream to her and she said, laughing, that she had better go home to prevent that scene from happening. Then, other talks followed and, around midnight, she did indeed have her head resting on my chest. We were totally in love with each other without having discussed it frankly in words. It was she who then reminded me of the dream I had told her earlier that night. We did not have sex that night. I accompanied her home around one o'clock in the morning and in the next forty-eight hours that followed, she returned to the university campus of Barmous, in Babiville, where she was staying. I was to visit him in the days that ahead.

It was in her narrow room in the student accommodation that we made love for the first time. It was sublime. Dalia was the most perfect woman I had ever known. She was delicate and everything about her was sheer delight. We could have eaten each other up that night, literally and figuratively, as we were on the same wavelength. I don't think I have ever spent a more memorable night than that first night of love in her small campus room. Although her single bed was so narrow, it seemed even too big for us. If it had been possible to shrink it further so that we were even closer together, we would definitely have reduced it by half. It was an absolute fusion of two bodies, the same thought, such concomitant heartbeats, the very breathing seemed unique and the embraces that did not leave a thousandth of space between us.

The next morning, we did not even have time to take a shower or brush our teeth. It would be much time spent away from each other. We woke up kissing passionately and it was like that all day long. And we continued to make love as much as possible, interrupting our antics only to say words of tenderness and express the outpourings of our hearts. That was the day we realised that Hollywood movies do not lie about that where actors wake up after a night of love and start kissing again without even brushing their teeth. We too had known that, that unique episode of total fusion between two people madly in love with each other. Soon after, I was going to start asking Dalia to marry me.

Disappointingly enough, each time I asked her to marry me, she would dodg the subject, saying that we were the same age and that, moving forward, she would certainly age before me and that I would give her up for a woman younger than herself. I found that argument particularly flawed. Finally, I thought I had the right end of things when she became pregnant with my baby on February 12th, 1995. At my master's dissertation defence at the Amphitheatre LB on March 25th, 1995, she honoured me with her presence by acting as my wife. She was gorgeous that day, as usual. On top of that, she was pregnant with the fruit of our love. A little being was being formed inside of her and I was happiest dad to be on earth. I thought that we would both become parents of a child who would be flooded with love each and every day in his life.

But the following week, Dalia came to visit me in Garbour. I wanted to eat her up like a dish again when I came across what was to destroy my life : she was wearing some kind of bandage following an abortion she had just done. She had killed our baby, the fruit of our love, without telling me! She knew very well that I would never have consented to getting rid of that unborn baby that I so badly wanted. And since I had proposed to her for the past two years, I was hoping that luck had finally smiled at me because she was already the mother of Sylvia, born out of wedlock. I knew she would never have wanted to become a mother of two children with different dads without her marrying either of them. I told myself that I was now on the right track. Anyway, with that abortion, I was shot in the heart. I believe I died that day. I was grieving for my son who had already died but much more, I was grieving for myself. I no longer existed. Dalia's stay in Garbour that time, in the beginning of April 1995, was the saddest of all. We spent every night together, as was customary when she ever came to Garbour. Her daughter Sylvia would come to my house very early in the morning to visit her mother. We were a nice family. We were not rich but we were usually happy, very happy indeed, until tragedy struck our small family with the disappearance of our unborn son.

Something broke down between us though during that last visit by Dalia because of the unilateral action she took earlier. A deep chasm. My soul was hurt. That child of Dalia and I was the jewel in the crown; the crowning of a perfect and an intense love story. It was the cement that was going to unite us forever, forcing us to set up a home, a family, with Sylvia, her big sister. However, the child was no longer there. He would never be there again. He would never say ''dad'' to me and never call Dalia ''mom'' because his mother, who was supposed to protect him first, had gotten rid of him without his father being informed. I could have vetoed the abortion; I could have opposed her decision; I could have stood between them and save his life. Alas! I could not save his life. I could not help him. I was his father. I too had failed him badly for I did not save his life. The day his life was on the line, I was not there to help, I did not stop his mother from ending his life. I was not in Babiville and I did not intervene to save him. I was in mourning. I loved that child who was not yet born. I loved him with the infinite love I had for his mother, the beautiful Dalia Amar. I was eager to see him become that indelible link between his mother and I. Alas, he was no more! I was a broken man.

After Dalia went back to University, an ex-girlfriend of mine who was no longer even in Garbour, came to visit me on her way to her village. She had gone to Yopo in her village some twenty kilometres down the road, on the right-hand side coming from

Dilma. When she returned from there, it was dark and I offered her shelter for the night. We were lying in bed when, around midnight, out of the blue, Dalia, the love of my life, showed up. I could no longer deny the infidelity. Young Francesca was nineteen years old and she had no relatives in Garbour. Her big sister was certainly a primary school teacher in Garnia but it was two kilometres further down the road, in the direction of Dilma, further south. I still could not kick her out around one o'clock in the morning. The best, it seemed to me, was for the three of us to sleep without making love and, in the early morning, Francesca would still leave for Lakanga, leaving us alone. However, Dalia decided to go home that late at night, leaving us alone. I did not sleep that night. I thought that we were over with what had just happened. How would Dalia welcome me after such a disaster? My sleepless night was spent thinking about my defence, my excuses, the words that could have helped her swallow the betrayal. But above all, I was afraid of facing the delicate gaze of the love of my life. If she looked me straight in the eye, what would I have to say? If she had the bad face of the betrayed lover, who wants to end the relationship, would I dig deep in the earth and disappear therein? I was lost. And soon it was day break without me finding the right formula to appease her cold anger.

I admit that I sought the opinion of Dao Junior, a friend who was much older than myself. I had asked him what to do in such extreme circumstances and I even asked him to go with me to her house so that he could ask for her forgiveness on my behalf. All I can say about that is this : he gave me the wrong advice which I still regret having followed. He asked me not to do anything but to let Dalia, the love of my life, digest her anger before asking for her forgiveness. It was the mistake of my life. I still do not know why he gave me such a bad advice. I lost her that way, for lack of experience and wisdom. While I reflect on that story, I wonder if that friend of mine was not jealous of our love. I question whether he was planning to go behind my back to make a move on Dalia. That was how I lost her for good. I sinned against her by inexperience. Instead of running to her the very next day to humble myself and prostrate myself before her and beg her forgiveness, I convinced myself that we had to let her digest the shock of the betrayal first. I thought we would have meaningful discussions about the incident later on when she would have calmed down. It was the mistake of my life. I lived to regret it.

The following year, in Dilma, I taught a year thirteen class for the first time. I was then really excellent in my role as a literature teacher. *Les Fleurs du Mal* by Charles Baudelaire, *Les Soleils des Indépendances* by Ahmadou Kourouma and *La Tragédie du Roi Christophe* by Aimé Césaire were on the school curriculum and my text explanations dazzled my students. It was at Dilma Comprehensive School that I successfully passed my DEA postgraduate degree before enrolling in the same year on my doctoral course under the supervision of Professor Lézog Gérald. Soon I was to be recruited as a teaching fellow at the Becken University Institute. For that reason, I left Dilma in October 1996 for Becken, in the centre of the country. I was to stay there for three years before leaving my native country for Bingué.

Chapter 2

Student memories, or when we were filled with hope
And we thought we were invincible

It was in October 1988 that I entered the ENS. We all had a scholarship right from the start. The sixty thousand CFA francs per month we were getting were an unexpected financial windfall for children of the poor that we were. There were some two hundred of us training to become secondary school teachers. Many of us had graduated at more prestigious high schools than my Comprehensive School in Odelta. Some came from highly respected schools such as the Lycée Scientifique or the Mami Adja high school in Yamina, others from the Mami Faltaille high school in Bougainville. Still others came from the mythical Classic High Schools of Babiville or Becken. The rest of us, who had passed our baccalaureate in Odelta, in Bandalia, in Teugouala and other small towns in the country had an unjustified fear of our peers who had attended prestigious high schools.

Soon that fear would vanish like thin air after the first group assessments when Mrs. Nicole Vaschalde gave us the first text explanation grades on a poem taken from Victor Hugo's *Contemplations*. I then hit the high mark of 15 out of 20 with no trace of red pen from beginning to end on any of the four pages of my essay. She warmly congratulated me and the others took notice. It was a real boost in my self-confidence.

I was soon going to do it all over again by getting another 15 out of 20 in another text explanation relating to an extract from the *Cahier d'un Retour au Pays Natal* by Aimé Césaire. From then on, my reputation was solidly established because from that moment on, my self-confidence grew prodigiously. I understood that after all I had more than what was required to undertake graduate studies in literature. Above all, the most remarkable thing in my studies as a trainee teacher of French was that in 1991, while I was a trainee high school teacher in a popular district of Babiville, I realised that many students in their first undergraduate year were photocopying my old assignments listed above to learn them by heart, just to familiarise themselves with the technique of writing up a text explanation. My past papers were their prototypes of successful writing and it was a real source of pride for the young man of twenty-one that I was back then. I had originally handed over those papers to my good friend, Delgun - Biadoum Belkary nicknamed Delgun - so that he could read them and use them to improve his writing. Obviously, several others had borrowed and photocopied them without requesting permission from me to do so.

I remember that back in the day I was a real vocabulary buff. I owed that passion for words to my French teacher in year thirteen, Mr. Bandeloquent Youssef. He was someone who was never satisfied with the usual words that everyone knew and used. He was into lexical elitism and he shaped us so much that year of 1988. When we moved to higher education, it was above all my classmates who paid the price for my love for rare vocabulary. When a group of students had to make a presentation, I would prepare simple questions for them but with such an eclectic vocabulary that the comrades understood nothing of it. I remember that used to upset them a lot as they looked like idiots in front of everyone. I thus made some "enemies" among those who felt humiliated by my questions which confused them.

I had a thesaurus in which I specially learned this varied vocabulary and I used those new learned words in real situations such as group presentations. I remember what Dr. Yré, a senior lecturer specialising in African novel had confessed to me once that he did not know how come I knew those so rare vocabulary items.

In general, I really enjoyed - and even savoured - my student years at ENS. We were accommodated in the student accommodation complex of Ababa II which was for single students. It is true that some students were married in those days. I did not study much and, to be honest, I never got into the habit of studying much anyway. I was just reviewing my lessons on the eve of each scheduled assessment. For the baccalaureate for example, I had reviewed my entire history lessons in a single day like reading a newspaper. The next day, I had read all the content of the geography lessons, and so on. My entire revision for the exam lasted seven days for the seven subjects we faced for the baccalaureate. On the eighth day, I passed the exam with flying colours. The same was true for the probationary baccalaureate. I have always operated on that lazy revision model. As I have mentioned, I never needed to summon more than ten percent of my intellectual capacities throughout my primary, secondary and higher education.

In higher education, my revision technique has hardly changed : I slept the day before each exam from five or six p.m. I would wake up at around 11:30 p.m. or midnight to revise from midnight to 6 a.m. all the content of the lessons related to paper to be examined in the morning. I would take a shower and leave for the ENS or University to sit the exam. I remember that for the bachelor degree, the master's degree or the DEA, I always did exactly the same. When there was a four-hour essay to write, I did not write any drafts. I would take five minutes to explain the subject to myself in simpler terms. I would think carefully about my introduction and my conclusion for half an hour. I would then take almost an hour to write up my essay directly on the exam paper without making any erasures or mistakes. I was blessed with a beautiful handwriting from childhood to the point where some of my classmates praised me for being a *"writer"*. It was their way of saying that I had a beautiful handwriting in the sense of calligraphy.

During exams, I would leave the examination room after an hour and a half. Some of my classmates thought that I obviously had not understood anything about the examination paper and that I was throwing in the towel before slipping away. They could not have been more wrong. I passed them all with ease.

For the postgraduate degrees like the mater's and the DEA degrees, I remember that I got, in a consistent way, the best mark in my class in dissertation with 14 out of 20. I guess the professors would not give me more than 14 out of 20 in dissertation or in various forms of essay. If they could award anyone a whooping 20 out of 20, surely I would have gotten them. Generally speaking, I know that my exam and other assessment papers came back to me without the slightest trace of red ink for that would suggest that the examiner spotted mistakes in the paper. There was nothing badly expressed nor a lack of accent in most of my dissertations. I mostly made no spelling or grammar mistakes of any kind when I wrote. I undoubtedly also owe a debt of gratitude to Dr Amissa Urbano who was one of our lecturers in the second year undergraduate course at the ENS. He had just returned from France and he liked to give us assignments strictly limited to writing an introduction or a conclusion only, or both, without the need to write up a development. I remember that I understood his motivation back then because I knew that the introduction was essential in any essay writing, and the conclusion too. I understood that if the examiner limited their reading to those two ends of an essay, they had to be convinced enough of its quality to award it an excellent mark. However, some of my comrades have never been able to excel in that sort of assignments. They were lost for ideas and did not know what to write. They would consistently get mediocre grades. In such exercise, I was always the best in my tutorial group for I always got a 3 out of 5 in each of those assessments. I must stress that Dr. Amissa Urbano never rated anyone 4 or 5 out of 5. On the other hand, he used to hand out many ones out of 5.

The most important event though that rocked my student years was undoubtedly what happened from February 19th, 1989. Kamani Affa Béatrice had just told me that day that she was pregnant with my baby. She was already four weeks gone. We had had an intimate relationship a month before - to the day - during our first meeting. She was truly my very first girlfriend ever. At that announcement, I panicked to such an extent that I no longer knew where to turn. I was afraid of becoming a dad at nineteen, with no love experience nor life experience at all. I did not know how to inform my extremely conservative Muslim parents. They would surely not understand why on earth did their nineteen-year-old son impregnate a young girl outside wedlock instead of pursuing his higher education. I feared their reaction of indignation and disappointment. I then lost my will to live and soon my classmates in the tutorial group were asking me questions. They wanted to know what was wrong with me as I had suddenly become so taciturn and quiet in class. Everyone had noticed that I was isolated, completely withdrawn from the group, thoughtful and dreamy. I no longer followed classes with the concentration that I was known for. My academic performance had started to suffer. I had become very quiet and I no longer spoke in class, neither during lessons nor between lessons. I did not speak to anyone. I was traumatised at the idea of becoming a dad and I was terrified of having to tell my parents. Besides, I did not know in what language I would tell them about what I had done.

Sometimes, I would imagine the birth of a son or I would consider having an abortion. It was not the means that I lacked to do so. I had my scholarship of 60,000 f.cfa per month and I could have financed such a disastrous operation. The only thing was that, should I choose such a tragic path, I wanted a professor of medicine to perform it, not an ordinary doctor, nor a n amateur in some illegal surgery. The latter ones used to performe that kind of procedure with the most dramatic consequences all over the country. Besides, having gotten someone else's daughter pregnant at eighteen, I did not want to add salt to their injury by risking the baby mother's life.

I had to summon my courage to explain to my comrades the predicament that I had put my girlfriend Béatrice and myself through. They had set up a special committee that came forward to discuss my worries. I really appreciated the concerns of the classmates for my welfare and mental health. I felt the need to talk to someone. I explained everything to them as they listened to me attentively. They cheered me up by telling me it was not the end of the world.

Béatrice was the daughter of a police officer whose police accommodation was close to the student accommodation complex I was staying in. I was in my first year at the ENS and I wanted to have a girlfriend like my fellow students who were more experienced than myself in those things of the heart. I remember that I asked Patricia, the girlfriend of a friend of mine, Thierry Louis to connect me with one of her friends. In our jargon, that meant introducing me to a friend of hers that I could ask out. The following days, she introduced me to Béatrice who had just turned eighteen and had even less sexual experience than me. Although she had celebrated her eighteenth birthday that month of January 1989, she looked far younger. You could easily give her sixteen years of age. She had known only one sexual partner before me and then, with her second lover, she was to become a mother. I especially felt sorry for her.

I will never forget the day when, in March 1989, I saw Béatrice, her sisters and an aunt came into my student room. I lived on the second floor, in room 632 B of building E of the student accommodation complex. I immediately understood the purpose of their unexpected visit before anyone opened their mouth. I was asked just one question :

- ''Mr. Bamba, do you know Béa?'', the older woman asked me.
- ''Yes, she is my girlfriend'', I answered.
- ''Ah good ! She is your girlfriend? Do you know she's pregnant?'' asked the lady who would be introduced later on as an aunt to my girlfriend.
- ''Yes, I know that she is pregnant with my baby since January'', I acknowledged.
- ''As you admit that you got her pregnant, we will not make a big fuss about it. At least you recognise that you are the father of the baby she is carrying. What we ask of you is that you take care of the pregnancy. She is almost three months pregnant already. She needs to start her maternity ward visits. You will have to give her money to go to the hospital for her first check-up'', the aunt added.
- ''How much does it take to do a maternity ward visit?'' I asked.

- ''You need 15,000 f.cfa'', the aunt replied.
- ''Never mind, here are 15,000 francs. Let her go for her first consultations right away'', I concluded.

Béatrice was completely silent throughout the whole talk as she was overwhelmed by the five or six people who had accompanied her to my room. She was no doubt ashamed to be at the centre of the scandal that was unfolding before her eyes. The whole group then left me after we had come to an agreement. I guess they went on to report to Béatrice's parents, her policeman father and her mother who had not come to confront me in my student accommodation.

A few days later, I was called to the home of Béatrice's parents and that exercise was the one I dreaded the most. I was accompanied by my friend Thierry Louis, who offered me moral support and acted as my spokesperson. I also needed a witness, or a bodyguard in case someone was planning to physically assault me. The meeting went badly, very badly indeed. Béatrice's mother was a dark-complexioned woman. Her heart seemed to be even darker than her skin. Moreover, she was a little bit overweight and her gaze was very unfriendly. She looked sideways as if she was unable of looking me straight in the eye. There was so much animosity in her eyes that I almost immediately regretted having answered their summons. Her eyes were devouring me as she spoke with such anger that she could not help but cry her heart out, accusing me of having destroyed her little girl's life. The other members of the family did what they could to calm her down. I can say it at this hour, I had a very bad time in her house.

In April and May 1989, Béatrice visited me to collect more money for her hospital. I remember that during her last visit in May, she informed me that she would be leaving Babiville to follow her parents to Essan where her father had been transferred. I have not seen her again for the next twenty-four years. I knew that she had given birth to a son on October 16th 1989 in Essan. They had written to me to announce the birth of the child and I was asked to send my identity card to allow the family to establish the birth certificate of the child, which I did. Alas, Béatrice's parents ignored my ID card as well as they ignored the name I had chosen for my son. He was given a totally Baoulé sounding name according to his mother's ethnic group. They were from the Baoulé tribe in Toumodi. In the end, the baby was called Kamani Kwassi Franck as I was to find out some twenty-four years later. They had written on his birth certificate : unknown father!

As soon as I emerged from that stormy meeting at my in-laws' house, unscathed, I swore to myself never to set foot in there again. I was finally reunited with my son twenty-four years later and we now have a normal relationship. In the meantime, a wall of ice had been erected between Béatrice's parents and myself. A mutual distrust, almost an animosity which hardly encouraged me to ever go back to theirs hoping to see the baby in Essan. However, much later on, when I really became an adult and was living in Bingué, I strived to find my son. In 2003, I decided to seek the help of Radio Ébrounia. I had that national radio station read a press release appealing to my ex-girlfriend to get in touch with me as soon as possible. I had all my personal details read on national radio as I sought to find out the whereabouts of my son. The objective was to find my son and negotiate with his relatives from his mother's side so that I could bring him to Bingué. His maternal uncle - who was a primary school teacher - had listened to my press release read on the radio and had spoken to his sister, Franck's mother. Béatrice herself paid attention as she listened to the next announcement on the radio the same evening and over the next two days too. However, she did not lift a finger on the grounds that the child's grandmother was refusing to hand over her grandson to the Diulas!

Finally, on January 1st, 2013, I prayed to the Lord asking him to find my eldest son for me, whatever his name was because I did not even know the name that the Baoulés had given him. I asked Jesus to find him wherever he was and to send him to me so that he would be the first to confess that I was his father. Eight months after that prayer, my son found, by pure accident, the maternity notebook that his mother had twenty-five years earlier. He read my name on there, his father's name, which had never been mentioned to him. He had always been told that his father denied him. He was then staying in Doukou, a medium-sized town in the West of Ebrounia. He looked up my name on Facebook and found me almost immediately. He then had a basic mobile phone that was not even an android phone. It was the simplest – and the cheapest - device that could be found on the market at the time. He got in touch with me on social media saying that it looks like I was his father. I had asked the Lord in my prayers eight months earlier, from January 1st, 2013 to make the events turn exactly that way. I had just been granted that favour by the Most High. The names of his mother, of his grandmother, of his grandfather, the day and place of his birth, all of that fit perfectly with what I knew about my son and his maternal family. This is how we met when he was already twenty-four years old. It was all thanks to divine intervention.

Chapter 3

My son, beware of the seduction of young girls, for there is nothing more ruinous for a man than a beautiful young woman with a heart of stone.

I have never tasted alcohol in my entire life nor did I try out drugs. In fact, I had only seen drugs on television or in Hollywood movies. Otherwise, I have never seen drug up close in real life. My only vice – if everyone had to have one – was that I liked women a little too much. It started at Odelta Modern High School when I was fifteen years old. I was in year ten back then and I was madly in love with Jolita Kounda, who, in my eyes, represented absolute perfection. She was beauty personified and was very fair-skinned, with regular facial features, large brown eyes, thick reddish lips without lipstick. Her hair was long and the curve of her shoulders was perfect. Her cheeks were absolutely symmetrical and equally filled without being plump or emaciated. Her height was average as befits a woman - by my personal standards of beauty. We were absolutely the same age although at that age she was still behind in her formal education as she was still in year six while I was taking the secondary education certificate. Jolita was extremely well built. Her thighs were full and her buttocks were simply out of this world, full, plump, fairly spread out without being overly huge. They gave her a very feminine gait. I loved her to bits and she knew that I deeply loved her even though I found it very difficult to tell her to her face. I believe that I declared my love to her in an extremely well-calligraphed letter. It was a real piece of poetry in prose. I naively waited for her to come and tell me that she understood my message and feelings and that she agreed to go out with me.

I remember that sometimes I went to see her and to ask her to give me my answer. She would tell me then that she would give me an answer soon and I contented myself with that promise which really meant nothing. I understood years later on that she was just as interested as me in us having a romantic relationship, but she expected me to take my responsibilities as a man who should take the lead in those matters. Back in the day, in Africa, girls would not take the lead in romantic relationships. They would let boys and men do all the talking and chasing up. It was deemed inappropriate for a girl to show an interest in a boy. Therefore, she should hide her feelings until the boy did his best to convince her and steal her heart. It took me an awful lot of time to get to know how women mentality worked in those intimate things.

Nothing speaks better of my inexperience with girls at the time than the evening I met Jolita not very far from her home in 1986. We were both sixteen then. She had dropped out of school while I was in year eleven. We walked together to my bedroom. I locked the door behind us and hugged her. I started asking her for my answer again and she claimed she would do it in writing. I found her a pen and some piece of paper to write on. I was waiting for her to write on it whether she agreed to be my girlfriend or not. She wrote nothing. I did not know what she wanted. I wanted her agreement, her full consent before attempting to do anything to her.

After a while, I very hesitantly started to unbutton her shirt. It took me a good two minutes to undo a single button. I was watching her body language closely to see whether she was consenting or not. She had a magnificent chest. Her skin was extremely fair and soft. She looked like a mix-raced girl. I had undone three of her shirt buttons out of six, which took me a whooping six minutes. When I saw her generous and most beautiful breasts on display so close to my eyes, I hardly dared touch them without her explicit agreement. She was bra-less and, quite frankly, there was absolutely no need for a bra anyway with such beautiful and firm breasts that she had! I stared at her for a long time to find out if she would forbid me to go any further, or if, on the contrary, she would allow me to remove the last buttons and move on to more serious business - or naughtier things, no doubt. I stared into her eyes to try read a sign of encouragement or censure.

Her face was sublime and luminous. I could not bear her so beautiful and so delicate gaze. Her big eyes disconcerted and disarmed me every time our eyes met. Her hair was straight and thrown back. Ah, her lips! I had never seen anything so pretty in my whole life as Jolita Kounda. After such a long and idle wait, she ended up getting impatient and put her buttons back on. I concluded that, obviously, she did not want to go any further. I began to plead again for her to give me my long-awaited answer which had already been delayed for two years and counting. We stayed in that locked room for more than two long hours without anything happening, absolutely nothing at all, not even a treacherous kiss. Tired of the waiting game, Jolita asked for permission to go home. I then opened the door and walked her home, still requesting my answer. In vain. I had to wait for that same answer for the next three years. All I can say about that was that I was probably the most patient boy in the business of romantic conquest. I could spend seven long years of my life courting the same girl without tiring.

When I customarily married Kyria on July 30th, 1998 in Becken, I had no idea that I was signing my death warrant, so to speak. After living together for only five months, our relationship became very rocky to the point where I separated from her and I sought a divorce. I had asked my uncle to go and hand her over to her parents but he firmly opposed such request for a divorce. His argument was that my request for a divorce came after so little time spent together. My uncle Yayous in particular interceded as long as he could to bring me back to my senses. He even travelled from Babiville to Becken to plead for the return of my wife to the marital house after three months of separation. It was because of all that family pressure that I had granted Kyria a second chance as of March 15th, 1999.

Soon after, she became pregnant with our first daughter together, Salma. However, we would soon be separated again for almost five and a half years because of my trip to Bingué. I had to get my papers before considering having her come join me overseas, which I did on June 14th, 2005. It was my death warrant I signed that day. Soon she began to have intimate relations with my brother Becqueu even in my own house. In less than a year of stay in Bingué, my good wife began an illicit relationship with the latter. Moreover, he was a false brother who had been jealous of me since our school years. We were classmates since year one in 1974 in Birgouin and we attended high school together in 1981. We did the same classes of years seven, eight, nine and ten. Some academic years, he would sit on the same bench as me. Well, that was before he got expelled from high school after year ten without the BEPC, the secondary school general certificate. In the meantime, I continued in year eleven with the BEPC diploma. Later on, I became a secondary school teacher while Becqueu had become a street vendor in Adjamtalla, a popular and commercial district of Babiville.

Years later, when we met again in Bingué, we used to do everything together. We walked together, we went shopping together and we visited each other all the time. He ended up marrying in 2004 a very ugly and older Portuguese woman, who was much older than himself. The rush into marrying her was motivated by his will to escape the threat of repatriation to Ebrounia. He chose me to be his witness as he married that woman at the register office. That was how he was able to stay in the country on the grounds that he was married to a European citizen. His real African wife, Marianne, and her son, Ousbecq, had stayed in Ebrounia. Later on, when he brought his son to Bingué, with my help, his white wife did not really want the boy in her house. So, he entrusted me with taking his boy in my house and I became his guardian, so to speak, for three years spanning from 2007 to 2010. During that time, Kyria was sleeping with Becqueu behind my back and in my bed each time I left Tourville to go teach in the schools of Northamia or in Luther. My children were in the village primary school and the house was theirs alone. I had to ignore that big secret for at least ten years.

It was on Sunday, June 12th, 2016 that the world was going to collapse around me. That day, Kyria had had very severe palpitations. We felt that she was going to leave us any minute. We had to ask her to confess anything she wanted to, just in case the worst happened. As I was afraid of hearing horrible things, I went for a pee before coming to listen to her confessions. While I was there, I heard a voice saying to me :

- Ask her, she committed adultery!

I was stunned. Kyria always told me - and I always believed her - that she had never known any other man but me. I was the only man in his life and I believed her. Where did the idea that she cheated on me come from? And who would she have done that with? When did such act of adultery occur?

I returned to find Kyria in the marital bedroom and asked her directly the essential question in the following words :
- ''Kyria, did you commit adultery?'', I asked.

- ''Yes'', she replied, bursting into tears.

I was confused and shocked. I was choking and shaking on my feet. A few moments later, I summoned up all my courage to speak again :

- ''Since when did you cheat on me?'', I asked.
- ''Last year, on June 12th, 2015'', she replied.

The incident of her severe palpitations took place on the anniversary of the fault. To the day. I wanted to know more :

- ''With who did you do that?'' I asked her.
- ''With a Zimbabwean'', she replied.
- ''What is his name ? And where did you meet him?'' I asked him eagerly.
- ''His name is Traton, Traton Muambe. I met him where I work as a cleaner in the evenings'', she acknowledged.

I understood things better then. She had a cleaning part-time job in the evenings at the headquarters of the Compagnie Nationale des Chemins de Fer - CNCF -in Bardamia. She explained to me that the man was a contract computer scientist and that he often came over to carry out some IT work in those offices on behalf of the computer company he worked for.

One evening though, when he was working on a computer in an office that Kyria had to clean, she was attracted to that man. She found him very handsome and attractive to the point where she was devouring him with her eyes. The man noticed her manners and ended up asking for her name and mobile phone number. She claimed she had refused to give him her number, but offered to take his anyway. She then got his number. She told me that she folded the piece of paper where he had written his phone number down and put it in the right pocket of the blue shirt of her work uniform. That same evening, she called him from her mobile phone and gave him her own number, which she had refused to do some two hours earlier.

The talks of infidelity followed and soon after she was getting into the BMW 3 series that I had given her to return to her work place at around 11:00 p.m. to chat with him. Meanwhile, I stayed in my room upstairs planning my French and Spanish lessons for the next day. I thought she was downstairs in the living room, watching television but, to my amazement, she was with her lover. The two were loved up in my car. They were kissing; he felt her breasts; he put his hand under his panties and put his fingers in the private areas he should not have access to. According to her, on Friday June 12th, 2015, they ended up making an appointment to spend the night together, knowing that I worked weekend nights in Julien Lévêque's warehouse in Bardamia. That part-time job brought me an extra €1,200. each month in addition to my income deriving from the teaching profession.

She picked him up that evening by car while I was having a nap in our bedroom before my nightshift. She dropped him off at our neighbourhood hotel and the two committed adultery together right there. Then she came home and when I left the marital home for work that night, she went back to meet him at the hotel and they made love again until four or five in the morning. She came back to sleep in our marital bed before I came home at around quarter past six in the morning. It was just too much for me to bear. I had heard enough. I could not fathom what she disclosed that day of infamy. How could she have deceived me as early as a year ago to the day? After all, this was someone who had loudly sounded the trumpet of faithfulness for nearly twenty years. She had proclaimed for eighteen years in a row that she had never cheated on me, even swearing it in front of pastors. I realised that I never knew my own wife. She was a stranger to me, with very dark secrets that I never suspected nor knew about. I understood that that act of unfaithfulness was certainly not the one and only time such an abomination had happened. I understood that God was not wicked enough to punish anyone's first mistake, but rather that he only exposes sinners who harden themselves in their abominations.

I urged her to confess to me the other faults of adultery because if she had had the courage to deceive me after seventeen years of marriage, she had not taken such a bad habit after having practiced virtue for so long. It was clear to me that this act of adultery was the continuation of a very long series of infidelity. I cooked it for a whole week, day and night, from Sunday June 12 to Sunday June 19, 2016. I did not leave to teach all week. I didn't work at Julien Lévêque on weekends either. I stayed in the room with Kyria to listen to her confessions. I thus knew that there had been other lovers, since 2001 in

Ebrounia, when my daughter Salma had barely walked. I learned that one of my former students, Perfide Yacoubou, had made my wife his mistress in Ababa while I was struggling to obtain my residence permits to bring her to Bingué.

I also learned that a certain Eric, who worked in the Western Union office where Kyria made withdrawals from my money orders, had ended up making her his mistress. I also learned that a Guinean from the Black Market in Adjamtalla, a certain Lacina, who was a twin, was dating Kyria and had impregnated her twice and that they had passed the pregnancies for fear that a big scandal break out and send my wife away. I also learned that she had had another affair with a young man who was a 8th grader in 1999 while Kyria and I were married and I had been a teacher for eight years already. I knew that she had linked up with another man, a bété, who would be arrogant and who was trying to impose himself on her. But I had to know other things, other illicit affairs like her love for a rich, crippled man who was in a wheelchair but also had a big black car with a driver.

This man came to pick her up at my friend Delgun's in Ababa-Andor for lunch to go and eat with her in the expensive restaurants in the business district, the River Plate, right in the center of Babiville. Imagine what followed these lunches between lovers! There was also Battara, my friend Delgun's colleague and neighbor who slept with her in hotels since he was married and he and his family lived in the same building as Kyria and my children, Salma and Joshua. But there was also another neighbor, who passed for a devout Muslim, with his eternal boubou on his back, who went out with her. Apparently, he met my wife when he came to buy the ginger juice that Maria, Delgun's wife was selling.

However, years later, even after I had brought her to me in Bingué, I was later to find out that a Nigerian, presumably a drug dealer, and whom the binguist police were actively looking for, was also dating Kyria. for €130 or €180 the pass. She was then nursing my son Moualid, who was only seven or eight months old. It was during the same period that she became pregnant with Karla. She never knew if I was really the father of the latter or if it was her Nigerian client who was the biological father. Karla was already seven years old and her mother jealously guarded this heavy secret. And to think that this woman sang urbi et orbi that she had known only one man in her entire life! She repeated it to me over and over again, told it to her fellow women. She even professed it in front of pastors. What impudence in the lie! What sacred countenance in falsehood and in deliberate lying? I then understood that some women could look you straight in the eye and solemnly announce that they were virgins when they had already given birth six or seven times! But the straw that broke the camel's back was his affair with Becqueu.

Of all the men who had dishonored her, I forgave her not this one. It was too much. She had gone too far by sleeping with my brother from the village, in my room, while my children slept next door. It seemed that their first intimate encounter took place in October 2006, at my house, while I was in Ebrounia for a short stay.

Of all the betrayals, this was by far the most painful, because it was with my brother Becqueu. Still going to cheat on me with some Zimbabwean who was totally unknown to me, but cheat on me with someone so close? Someone in my intimacy? A man with whom I would be forced to live all my life and at whose funeral I would have to attend? Or who will have to come to mine if I were to go first? Human language has produced no words that can convey the pain I felt about this. I understood then what men meant when they said they suffered in their soul. Because this suffering is hardly in the flesh, but in the depths of our humanity, that is to say precisely in our soul. The suffering at this level of depth is far more excruciating than that which one can feel in one's flesh, when one is injured or burned by fire. It is a pain that tortures and gnaws at you from within while your physical appearance seems intact.

PART FIVE

THE OTHER SIDE OF THE MEDAL

Chapter 1

When you are an asylum seeker, to cease being
a human being to morph into a migrant

Asylum seeker, this is how we were indexed. Asking for asylum. Sometimes we were called illegals, or illegal migrants, undocumented. It wasn't so much that we didn't have papers, but we didn't just have binguist papers. We had our birth certificates and our national passports which counted for nothing in this country of Bingué. Me, I also had all my diplomas from the CEPE, the certificate of primary education, to the DEA. But I was still undocumented. I also had my vaccination card, my blood group card, my national identity card and other identifiers. All were confiscated from me at the South Terminal of Garrick Airport on Friday, August 6, 1999 at around 6:30 a.m., with the exception of my diplomas and a copy of my master's thesis.

I was therefore undocumented like so many thousands of others. When you are undocumented, you cease to be human simply to become a migrant. The migrant is someone strange, who comes from elsewhere, from very far from home, and who comes to dispute the bread with our young children. The migrant is therefore a threat, a threat coming from someone we do not know and who is constantly on the move. The migrant comes from afar, has travelled a lot and is looking for a place to stay with us. It represents a potential threat and the media are responsible for conveying this idea on all their platforms: on television, in newspapers, on the radio, on the internet, we only talk about migrants, asylum seekers and invasion of Bingué of which they are guilty.

Sometimes when we work with the native white binguists, they ask us what we came to do in their binguist islands. We are forced to tell them that we came there to study, which immediately calms them down, knowing that we have come from so far away to learn in their excellent universities. But the question that invariably follows is how much longer will our classes take. If we tell them that we have two years of study left, or one year, they are really relieved but they always ask what we plan to do after our studies. Are we going to go home after our studies? Often they go directly to the essential question:

- When are you going home?

The life of migrants is a dog's life! It is an execrable pedigree marked by suspicious and oblique glances, the animosity of the natives, the indignant denunciation of the opposition parties, the hostility of the media, the latent racism of the populations of origin.

in this country of Bingué, eighteen years later. It is the place of the most abject uprooting: you are never really integrated for real in this country of Bingué and you no longer really have any ties to your country of origin either. Our parents can die without us being able to go to their funeral. One can lose all one's uncles and aunts after an extended illegal stay which runs for twenty or thirty years. We lose our African mentality and embrace Bingué's mentality. We become a kind of wood which, by dint of staying too long in the water, thinks we are a caiman.

Asylum seekers are migrants just like the desert locusts that infest a state and eat all its crops and even its green leaves and grasses in a few days or weeks, before vanishing into the wild. Except that in the case of migrants, they stay there for a long time to nibble on the public funds of the country of Bingué. Many of them benefit from social assistance for the unemployed because their professional situation is very precarious. They do small jobs, menial jobs that the natives of Bingué would never agree to do. They are thus cleaners, or surface technicians for those who have the improving vocabulary. They are found in all the train stations in Bingué with buckets, cleaning products, plastic gloves and stereotypical clothing combinations. They are also found in public toilets, near the toilets in Bingué airports, in schools at the descent of classes and in offices. They often carry black trash bags. They work between two and four hours in offices and schools, while in train stations and airports, it is almost a full-time job: eight hours of hard work a day.

They are also found in the functions of security guards. They are even sometimes promoted to dog handlers. They then hold a dog on a leash, drive it home, and spend the night with it. This dog is then the guarantee of their work. They train it to perform a specific task and it is part of their life.

Migrants are people with little ambition. They just want to live next to their hosts and lead a quiet little life without making too much noise. They want to earn their daily bread, as they say, by lowering their heads, and make some transfers of money to the country of origin to satisfy the voracious demands of relatives left behind. These parents, real leeches sometimes, harass them with requests for money to such an extent that one would think that they would all starve if the money order had not arrived the same day.

The lives of migrants are also reduced to working hard, not sleeping enough, eating poorly, sending money home and remaining without savings in Bingué. Rarely do they resolve to study, thinking that the years spent on the benches of training schools or universities are so many dead losses in financial terms. They don't even have time to learn Bingué's language to master it well enough. Sometimes, when it comes to reading in the Bingué language, or filling out forms in this language, they call on other people. Some migrants stay in Bingué for ten or twenty years without being able to read and write properly. For all the needs of social life, such as reading an administrative letter, or responding to it, they called on scribes. For court appearances, they need translators. The life of a migrant is life at a minimum. He may not work and be content with housing assistance and unemployment assistance. It's just having a roof to sleep under and putting something in your stomach when you go to bed.

This is also a point on which migrants are attacked in the press and by political parties in opposition to Bingué, especially in the run-up to the general elections. We rehash while migrants swarm on the coasts of Bingué like flies attracted by unholy smells. It is then argued that if social aid were not put in place, there would certainly be few migrants in the streets and neighbourhoods of Bingué. And this speech appeals to some people who complain about not being in the butter, living in council housing. Migrants are so publicly indexed as being responsible for all the ills that undermine binguist society that they hug the walls, hide or hide their identity as asylum seekers. Some claim to be French and not African to escape the stigma that sticks to the skin of African migrants.

I remember, for example, my comrade Fiston, who was an Ebrounian migrant who entered Bingué with a fake French identity card. He had gone by Eurostar from Gare du Nord to Saint Pelbès. He has always lived and worked in Bingué under this false nationality for at least seven years. He had been able to save up to €30,000, or nearly twenty million of our francs in 2009. One day he had a hard time wanting to get his driver's license. He sent his false French identity card to LAVDA, the agency that regulates the sector and which is based in Smirne, to obtain a provisional permit. Generally, it hardly takes a week to receive the provisional permit. But a month had passed without anyone answering him. He wasn't overly concerned. One day when he was at work in a warehouse in Fordia, what is called the djossi in popular language in Africa, the police arrested him for identity theft. He was handcuffed and locked up in Yarlovue detention center near Fordia.

At the same time, a team of police had come down to his house to search his room from top to bottom. His bank statements, bank cards and other confidential documents were discovered. Proceedings were opened against him for having kept criminal emoluments in his possession. His crime? Having worked under a false nationality, which is a crime and any salary received doing such work was considered to be from money laundering. It was like he was selling drugs. Finally, after a month's detention, he was tried and repatriated manu militari to Ebrounia and his fortune of €30,000 was donated to charities. This is how Sonny ended his life as a migrant. Stripped to the bone!

His older brother, Ludovic, smarter, had more luck than him. He had his head on his shoulders. He could neither read nor write. He did not bother to want to buy a car. He was content to own a bike that does not take any fuel, nor does it require a gray card, any more than a sticker or a driving license. He did not keep a penny in any bank in Bingue. Every Friday, he systematically repatriated his weekly salary to Ebrounia. After seven years, he wanted to return to his country voluntarily, without being expelled. He was already a business manager in his native country when his youngest, Fiston, was repatriated penniless. He only had his shirt on. But Ludovic had bought two heads of DAF trucks to send them to the country, with vans that we call gbakas at home and which are used for public transport between the different municipalities of the Babivillo metropolis. He had thus acquired a car park to set up a transport company of which he became the CEO.

When you are a migrant in Bingué, you have to have a lot of common sense and caution, live hidden like a serpentine in order to grow. The key is to avoid getting interested in anything related to owning or driving a car. Because it's very easy to get caught trying to get a driver's license or if you don't have insurance, if you're suspended from driving for a certain period of time, if you haven't paid the tax annual road traffic, or if the technical inspection is not up to date, or if your car has been damaged, or if you forget to pay a ticket for speeding or other traffic offences. If the illegal migrant commits some mistake related to his car, we snoop around his entire life, we undress him to see clearly his identity and his status as an illegal migrant or not. The consequences can be dramatic as Fiston has learned the hard way.

But migrants are sometimes daring too. Some try to stay in Bingué at all costs. Because it is a shame to be repatriated to your country of origin, without a suitcase, or a bank card, with just a shirt on your back. When we then pass through the streets, we are pointed out, like a repatriated binguist, who walks with sandals on his feet! This is how some of them go so far as to buy themselves husbands or wives who are European. They then make sham marriages, just to apply for a five-year stay with the services of the

Ministry of the Interior. The Portuguese had specialized in this trade around 2003 and the following years. They came from the poor regions of Portugal to marry an African migrant on the very day of their landing in Saint Pelbes. They wore a white wedding dress for the ceremony at the town hall, then changed clothes right after, then took Eurostar or Easyjet back to their country. There was no reception ceremony after the wedding. No more wedding night, just colour photocopies of their European passport, their identity card, the marriage certificate and some photos of the wedding ceremony. The contract cost an average of €4,000 for a Hollywood performance of no more than thirty minutes plus travel time there and back. What would a migrant not do to settle in Bingué? All prices were likely to be paid to stay in Bingué. At least you could work and get that money back on two or three months of hard work, even in menial jobs that didn't require any special qualifications.

However, some migrants killed themselves on the job. James, my Ghanaian comrade almost died like this. He alone had three employers, two of whom were in Fordia and one in Londamou. He had to do three jobs every day. He would finish one and go to the other place of work. After the first two day jobs in Fordia, he took the train to go to Londamou for the night job. His twenty-four hours of the day were busy working and commuting between employers. He returned to Fordia by train around four o'clock in the morning to resume his routine early in the morning. He slept during the thirty minutes of the journey between Londamou and Fordia. After several years of such work worthy of a medieval convict, he paid a visit to his native Ghana in 2012. He fell at Kotoka airport in Accra on the day of his return to Bingué. First, he felt dizzy. He saw as if the whole earth was rocking around him, violently shaken by some tsunami. He thought he saw the majestic waves of the Atlantic Ocean swallowing up terrain and hurtling dizzily towards the airport. His feet let go. He lost his balance, rocking like a drunken boat whipped by rushing winds on the high seas. His eyes had grown bulging and bulging. Only the whites of the eyes could be seen, for the pupils seemed to have disappeared under his eyelids. It was a frightening convulsion. James was having a sharp attack of fatigue accumulated in his man's body. Physiology finally reclaimed its long-scorned rights. He collapsed there, in front of everyone, with his legs moving frantically in a spasm like those of a chicken that had just been slaughtered. He benefited from a medical evacuation because he had very quickly sunk into a coma. It was a month later that he woke up from his sleep in a London hospital bed without knowing how he had failed there. James almost died that year. His physical body could no longer bear this burdensome galley.

When he saw his wife and children around him, in the blurry vision of a man returning from Hades, he understood the full tragedy of his situation. He could well have made a widow and orphans to want to work so hard to try to redeem the time and build villas in Accra, in the southwestern district of the capital in the direction of Ebrounia. This district was in the process of carving out the reputation of a district of binguists, that is to say where Ghanaian migrants settled in Bingué came to buy bare land which they developed by building sumptuous villas, respectable luxury duplexes, at the cost of their blood. Their Ghanaian compatriots, who knew nothing of the sacrifices of the Jameses at Bingué, imagined that money was collected there in the streets, as in Eldorado. They imagined that it was enough for a man to bend down to pick up gold in the streets of Bingué, without effort, to come and build great buildings in the country. If they only knew that it was at the cost of their sweat and their blood that these migrants, like beasts of burden, pulled the plow night and day to afford such investments! Migrants are no longer quite human beings; they are machines, robots programmed to work day and night, just like Bingué's factories and robotic warehouses, which run twenty-four hours a day.

Chapter 2

Naturalisation is the culmination of an administrative process and not the trigger for successful social integration

I always hoped that the intruder feeling would go away once I acquired binguist nationality. I think I was completely off the mark and I would soon find out. In July 2006, I ended up opting for this naturalization and I very quickly obtained my new burgundy red passport. I was over the moon when I acquired this naturalization because I really liked Bingué. I liked the binguist language and civilization. I liked the history of the country that I traveled extensively from Birful to Gailla to Bandor, Abertune, Barbaful, Nelport, Barbados, Lidantha, Berfulia, Lorgna, Sheriffa, Cherville , Moyenda, Hamford, Neuchastel, Glasnord, Ederfin, Dalford, Carambert, Fordia, Bardamia, London, Brigor, Charleville, Ghamford, Lemarford, Luthor, Svendia, etc. . I know the geography of the country and I like its varied landscape from the hills and mountains of the north country to the Gaillais meadows and the economic development of the south of Bingué. I like the highways which I know perfectly well having driven my nineteen cars there between 2003 and 2019. I like the train stations and the railways which I traveled regularly between 2000 and 2001 when I worked in the security industry to finance my doctoral studies. I loved this country with a sincere love as if it had seen me born.

But, once I became a binguist citizen, I realized that nothing had really changed in my situation. My job applications as a teacher-researcher in the universities of the country always fell through despite my new status as a citizen. I finally realize that naturalization is just the culmination of an administrative process and not the trigger for social integration. The Social Democrats were in power then and the economy under Prime Minister Beau Parleur was vibrant. But I was always ignored at the level of the universities where I aspired to be recruited.

I then resolved to stay in secondary education, visiting schools where a colleague was absent. It's less stressful at least and there are fewer corrections to make. The only challenge is that you have to adapt to each school where you set foot for the very first time and often only once in your life. You have to get along with students and colleagues from the first contact.

It's quite fascinating work in this sense because we acquire the art of making good contacts with others and leaving good memories from our first meeting so that the same schools call on us the next time they are in need. But there are also some schools that keep us on for the long haul, meaning for several months at a time, or for a term, a semester, or even an entire school year. This is how I was posted to the Seldom Campus in 2014-2015. It was a high school near my house. So it was convenient because I could eat at home at noon before returning to class for the afternoon lessons. I had a 5th grade class that was giving me a lot of worries. I must say that in reality, one of the students in said class was a difficult social case to manoeuvre. Charlie Lobb was a difficult child. He was kicked out of school almost every week or one or two days of school. So he had to stay home those days. Originally from Ebroun, I told him one day that I knew his father. Therefore, if he behaved badly in my classes, I would directly call his father who was the same age as me and report to him. I even mentioned his father's name and he was shocked. From that moment on, he had a hypocritically too profound respect for me. But I was not fooled because all the other teachers complained about him. He was the head of a gang called L'Équipe made up of about twenty rogue members. He was one of the youngest in this gang, only enrolled in 5th grade while the others were mostly in 4th or even 3rd. He was their leader and for good reason. By dint of undergoing the temporary exclusions, they no longer meant anything to him. Around March 2015, if I remember correctly, he was returning from yet another three-day suspension when he attacked a white 4th grader. Together with her classmates, they beat her violently at school and he knocked her off her feet. The poor girl fell to the ground and he jumped on her legs, breaking them with one blow. The police and the ambulance were called to help the unfortunate woman who was transported to the emergency room of the Bardamia University Hospital. Lobb was arrested that day and the school resolved to fire him for good. His normal school career ended there. He then joined a parallel structure reserved for child offenders excluded from the normal circuit. A few years later, he joined the real gangs outside and some of his comrades stabbed him in the stomach. His guts were out but his life was saved. Saved by the bell!

Unfortunately, this is often how children born to African migrants in Bingué end their panicked race to failure. Some of their parents are unable to follow their formal education. They cannot help them with the homework given by the teachers. Some of them just can't read. If they can still read a little, they have no intellectual capacity to control the quality of work done by their children and above all to guide them step by step so that they improve their work. Others work too hard like James, working two full-time jobs or even three concurrent jobs. They don't even have time to sleep four hours a day. So, don't ask them to make sure their kids are doing well in class or doing their homework to the best of their abilities. Yet these children born in Bingué are all binguists by nationality. Their parents have almost all acquired the nationality too, even if their level of language barely allows them to carry on a decent conversation.

This is the biggest drama of immigration: the school failure of the children of immigrants is so glaring that the internal statistics of the schools and the Government are alarmed by these poor scores that they achieve in the BEPC. The vast majority of them leave the normal circuit of education at this stage and cannot go to the second cycle of secondary school to do a baccalaureate or hope to go to university. They can't secure grades from 'very good' to 'fairly good' in both English, math and science to hope to go further. They are therefore obliged to go to vocational training schools, colleges, to clear their conscience. It is therefore not uncommon to see them accept jobs as cleaners like their migrant biological parents who have the excuse of being born in Africa, and who arrived in Bingué aged, without diplomas, with a very high level of foreign language. weak. They were born in Bingué; they have been to school in Bingué since kindergarten and speak the language with a native listener accent. However, they were sorely lacking in basic education at home and they never grasped the meaning of going to school, of getting a good education and getting a good job, of ending up as MPs or ministers. They work at McDonald's, Burger King or KFC after dropping out. Sometimes, they are also found in large numbers in warehouses as unskilled workers. They waste their lives in these menial jobs and end up founding, like their parents, disjointed and dislocated families. For them, as for their parents, it is clear that naturalization is the culmination of an administrative process and not the trigger for successful social integration. They remain on the margins of binguist society. They stay in their community and don't mix with whites anymore. They tear down the walls to maintain the social and racial status quo ante. They are devoid of ambition to move the lines. In high schools and colleges, it was these children of African migrants who posed the most problems for us. They were often insolent and did poorly in class.

Sometimes, their mom shamelessly cheated on their dad who kicked her out. Having become a single mother, she clung to the children to keep social benefits such as tax credits for children, housing assistance and unemployment assistance. They thus believed themselves to be millionaires and wasted their youth changing boyfriends as soon as they were freed from the patriarchy of a husband who dominated them. After the fifty years, when the freshness of the beauty had disappeared and they found themselves alone, it was total despair. The social aid they discovered in Bingué did not help their families; they destroyed them so much they exacerbated the appetites of each other. It is a permanent war which is declared between the parents for the control and the division of this money. Instead of it serving the advancement of children by putting them in the best conditions of life and studies, each parent can monopolize it to spend it on themselves. When the wife feels aggrieved in sharing the cake, she leaves the marital home with her children and claims that she is beaten or verbally abused by her husband. The town hall therefore found him immediate refuge, then permanent housing sponsored by the municipality. As she looks after the children, the money from social assistance is now paid into her account so that she can buy longer locks, longer boots that go beyond the knee!

When I obtained binguist nationality in August 2006, I was full of hope. I told myself that I would finally have all the good positions available in higher education here in Bingué. I figured that if a university wanted to recruit a specialist in French literature who was fluent in French, I would obviously be the best choice. I was sorry for having harboured so many false hopes because I was royally ignored by all the universities that wanted to recruit a teacher-researcher specializing in 19th century France. It took me eighty consecutive failures to realize that we certainly needed a man with my qualifications, but we certainly didn't need me. My PhD and my burgundy red passport changed absolutely nothing. I had to know my place and keep myself square. I had to stay in my place and be satisfied with little, just like my fellow migrants who had not formulated insane ambitions by aspiring to positions in binguist high society. These repeated failures reminded me of a well-known African proverb which says that not all sheep for sale at the market have the same price! I had been wrong to think that with my big diploma and my binguist nationality I had the same price as the other applicants, white and Asian. Apparently I had been wrong. Apparently, I had overstated my selling price on the academic labor market in Bingué!

The most mind-boggling situation I have experienced in this regard occurred in 2004. I had just completed my doctorate the year before. However, it happened that a college in Kempis where I had taught so many times, Collège Harcourt, wanted to recruit a French teacher to teach up to second grade. I applied for this position. Another was a candidate. He was white, a kid who was a student there a year or two ago, and who had dropped out after high school, before going to work in the travel industry at Voyages Plus. I found myself with him in the waiting room, reviewing my thirty-minute lesson that I had to do in front of the recruitment panel. He was surprised that I had prepared a lesson for the audition. Apparently, he didn't even know that we should give a French lesson in 4th grade for half an hour, in front of the head of the foreign languages department and a French teacher. I did my course in front of the two ladies who obviously appreciated it. Then he had to give his lesson which he had not even prepared. He could not express himself fluently in French either because his knowledge of the language was very limited. In addition, he had stopped his studies in 2nd class. How could he obviously teach this foreign language until 2nd grade? He had never graduated from high school, had never been to college, and had never taught in his entire life. He must have been eighteen!

Admittedly, I was a qualified teacher abroad as we say here in Bingué, because I was trained at the ENS de Babiville. But I had obtained a PhD in the discipline. I had taught French and Spanish in several schools in the region in 2002-2003 and I did the same in 2003-2004. But I failed for this kid was offered the holy grail. He was recruited without further ado as a French teacher. In 2005, I went back to the same school and I heard that the young man had quit after a term because he could neither prepare the lessons nor teach French to anyone. He suffered terribly at the hands of the students not only because he was too young and most of his students knew him from having been one of them a year or two before, but mostly because he knew nothing about it. to the French language. So he threw in the towel to get a job where he would have less stress!

This is how life is here in Bingué. We let certain skills pass because they are migrants, these sub-humans. On the other hand, we prefer to take the risk of trying novices and absolute blues in sensitive positions. We really wonder what the recruitment criteria are for us to come to such grotesque situations. But all the sheep that are on sale at the market do not necessarily have the same price, although they are all sheep. I ended up understanding the situation and knowing my own price.

This is undoubtedly one of the reasons why I decided, courageously, to leave Bingué to relocate to my country of origin. I figured I could make a difference there, by teaching at the university. I also felt that being bilingual would give me a certain advantage and that I could bring added value to my position as a teacher-researcher in French novels. I felt that having experienced teaching in Bingué, I could innovate teaching techniques in Ebrounia by using digital where traditional methods were still in force with markers and the whiteboard. Admittedly, I probably earn four times less money here than in Bingué, my monthly salary being equivalent to my weekly income there. But I have the satisfaction of working as a doctor and being recognized as such. I can finally demonstrate all my intellectual and professional qualities. I can move up in rank and finish my race with the rank of full professor.

My only regret is that I have already lost nineteen years of my life before making such a decision. Because in this period of time, I would have already climbed all the levels to become a teacher for about ten years. All those who are my bosses today at the level of my teaching unit have sometimes obtained their doctorate after me. I would have become a teacher before some of them. But I am happy to have finally started my university career alongside them. Humbly, I will learn alongside them. Because they have remained in constant contact with the scientific evolution of current techniques and concepts; they continued to conduct research, to supervise doctoral theses and to publish books and scientific articles where I remained static all these years. Suffice to say that I have stepped back over these past nineteen years. But I have plenty of time to buy back the time and finish a professor before retiring in twelve years.

When I retire here at sixty-five, I'll see if any binguist university would like to give me some five more years as a professor or visiting professor. Who knows if I won't make a full circle of my career?

Chapter 3

Communitarianism is the trademark of the degeneration of contemporary Western societies

The fundamental problem of binguist society, even of all Western society in general, is that of communitarianism. It is a mark of withering on its face which makes it descend into a certain degeneration. This is the plague of contemporary Western societies where we live next to each other, but we do not live together. We do not know the names of our immediate neighbors. We do not frequent them, especially if we are of different races or different religions. Muslims hardly make the effort to meet in mosques to share iftar together, the meal that ends the Ramadan fast each evening. Christians often meet at church just as co-workers meet at work every day. But no one associates with anyone outside of the mosque, the church or the workplace. The reports are distant, thus nourishing all illegitimate suspicions.

Black nationals from the African diaspora socialize with each other. Pakistanis hang out with each other. Indians do the same. The Chinese also live in isolation. White binguists live among themselves too. Communities live side by side. Even the Jews live in their neighbourhood north of Londamou, not far from the AM1 highway or in their neighbourhood in Neuchastel. The communities do not mix, communicate with each other or frequent each other.

Each of these communities lives in isolation, next to the other. We are neighbours, not friends. We tolerate each other but we don't really know each other to claim to love each other. The key to the system is good neighbourliness. As long as we remain good neighbours, no one complains. But if there is a crime that affects one community and the criminal is from another community, then the media reports clearly reflect the latent antagonisms between communities, the sly and veiled racism that no longer dares to be called of his name because of political correctness.

However, certain ethnic minorities - it is no longer fashionable to write racial, because that is racist - often provoke and upset these good neighbourly relations, as is unfortunately the case with the Muslim community of Luthor. Pakistani Muslims, who are very numerous in this city, do not miss any opportunity to parade in the streets shouting slogans very hostile to the police and the white indigenous binguist community, calling them khuffars - disbelievers - and cursing them. They throw them into hell in abject songs, in a diurnal way without the police being able to do anything, nor for that matter the political and administrative authorities. We are forced to let them do it in the name of democracy here in Bingué. But these people do not allow anyone to freely practice Christianity in their country under any circumstances. They would never allow anyone to walk the streets of Pakistan promising hell to Pakistanis and their police on the grounds that they do not believe in Jesus and therefore as disbelievers they would go to hell. Not content to freely practice their religion imported from the Middle East here in Bingué, they go beyond their rights and trample on those of the natives who have welcomed them with open arms on their soil. They treat them as unbelievers, promise them hell and go so far as to demand that the law of their religious faith, the sharia, be applied here in Bingué instead of the penal code of this country. They reject the legitimacy of the law and justice of this host country and demand that sharia be applied to all citizens of Bingué, whether they are Christians, Jews or without religion.

The situation has become almost untenable in certain parts of Londamou where the police are not welcome and where the binguist justice system does not sit and rule on cases that concern the Muslim communities of these neighbourhoods. They have established their own parallel justice system, sharia courts that deal with divorce cases within them and many other cases such as custody of children in divorce cases. Binguist law is totally flouted in these neighbourhoods and the authorities, preoccupied with electoral issues, turn a blind eye to these serious abuses which are causing an Islamic state to insidiously settle in the heart of Londamou and dictate its law there. It is as if binguists were going to settle in Islamabad or Riyadh and illegally set up courts there operating on the basis of binguist law in defiance of the sharia which governs social life in the Pakistani and Saudi states.

It is this kind of drift that risks weakening the current inter-community balance in Bingué. In the long run, I tell myself that this will cause serious problems for Bingué to the point that no one will know how to solve them. Habit will eventually become second nature. It is like certain individuals in these religious communities who publicly say and proclaim that they define themselves as Muslims first before considering themselves as binguists. Their loyalty is not to the state but to a religion imported from the Middle East. But they refuse to return to this distant land to practice their faith in the strictest sharia requirements. It is an attitude that I have always found paradoxical, especially coming from the most fundamentalist Islamic preachers, who encourage young people whose parents have migrated from this distant part of the world to come and settle in Bingué. When the government decides to strip them of their binguist nationality, they go to court, but not in their illegal sharia courts. They go to the legal courts to try to retain the nationality of those they consider to be hell-bent disbelievers. They vehemently oppose any attempt to return to their country of origin. They fight in the courts for years to avoid such a scenario.

However, I was shocked by the case of these three young girls of Pakistani origin, including Shamima Begum, who, at barely sixteen years old, got it into their heads that it was an excellent idea to gain paradise by going offer their charm and their youth to the extremist fighters of the Islamic State as "wives" without a dowry. For them, marrying bloodthirsty killers like ISIS warriors was the best way to contribute to the advancement of global Jihad. The fighters mostly needed sex, they said. And they were willing to offer it to them on a golden platter. Having spawned small jihadists in Syria, they now want to repatriate them to Bingué to go and destroy binguist society from within. It would probably be better for these little ones, born in Syria to jihadist fathers and mothers from the Middle East, to stay there to advance the cause of the IS caliphate.

It is the same logic that led Jihadi John to go into exile in Syria and to decapitate with a kitchen knife his fellow binguists or Americans who had the misfortune to drive trucks loaded with humanitarian aid for the benefit of Syrian civilians. Can you be born in any country, have grown up with your children and go and kill your children so cruelly in a third country? Even if we didn't have the recognition of the belly, couldn't we have humanity in ourselves? Because humanity knows how to show empathy. The natural man has compassion for his neighbour who is suffering or helpless. The natural man has enough compassion in him to rescue their neighbour whose life is in danger; he does not slaughter them! Nor can he decapitate them to please a distant God. Above all, he cannot perform such a barbaric act and legitimately think that it would lead him to paradise! Simply because if one has to slaughter their fellow human beings to carve out their way to paradise, what exactly would they have to do to go to hell? Shall we then have to do good deeds and save human lives to go to hell? It's hair-raising in the end! The whole ideology does not make any sense at all.

Suspicions between communities are undoubtedly even more exacerbated in the United States where each quarter, the media echo that a white policeman, or sometimes a white civilian, coldly shot a black man because he found him suspicious! It is still alarming to consider, when leaving home, that the colour of your skin constitutes a danger of death and that, because of this skin colour, you might never return home the same evening. That, no doubt, we would call our wife and our children in order to identify our body riddled with bullets at the hospital in the evening.

If we want to harmonize binguist societies in general, we should probably tear down the walls of communitarianism by encouraging living together. Living next door has sufficiently shown its limits. We should try to live together which would lead the ethnic and religious communities to blend into each other under the law voted in Parliament, and not under sharia or under the law of Moses. We would thus break the ghettos and the pernicious sects to allow the emergence of a better integrated society, less degenerating and less antagonistic. Some would get to know each other better, their culture and their vision of the world in order to live better with them.

Because if we knew each other better, we would love each other more and we would have less urgency to go and massacre our own neighbours in Syria with whom we would have shared so many things. I confess that I have never understood the validity of this disloyalty towards a nationality which one has freely requested and accepted; this treachery towards the fatherland which nourished, whitewashed and educated us. If we hate Bingué so much, why not settle in the Middle East and live in a vacuum, among Muslims, from generation to generation, without ever compromising its halal way of life? Why come to settle in the homeland of others when we know very well that this country cultivates religious, moral and political values that could potentially corrupt our holiness?

And then, speaking precisely of holiness, what is holy in cutting off the head of an innocent person for the sole reason that he is a citizen of a country that one hates? In what way are we holy if we sow death as a fingerprint everywhere we go? Is there really a God who loves death and slaughter so much to arrange the most excellent place in his paradise to house these bloodthirsty criminals?

I have always been shocked by the senseless murders that these people attribute to themselves. I was thus haunted by the murder of soldier Léon Rugby who had done no harm to anyone. The poor man was going home in the middle of Londamou when two of these fellows fell on him with shortened arms, machetes in their fists. And they hoped to trigger a holy war between their camp and the one they considered impure, the unbelievers, the native binguists. Naively, they really believed that the other Muslims of Bingué would take up arms and follow in their footsteps in the streets of the capital, to sow terror there.

But the height of horror was certainly reached on July 14, 2016 in Nice, among our neighbors, the Gauls. On the Bingué television channels, I followed, dumbfounded and mystified by the abject, unspeakable massacre of the Promenade des Anglais. One of these enlightened criminals was then driving a

19-tonne truck at high speed, deliberately ramming into the crowds. On his isotopic course of death, he was to leave behind him some eighty-six dead and four hundred and thirty-four wounded. It was the height! Can we imagine that there is the slightest depth of humanity in an individual who performs such an act? Because certainly, if we were human at least, we would be incapable of dreaming up such a scenario. But put it into practice, in the middle of a national holiday? To be guilty of such a totally indiscriminate massacre on the grounds that one loves a God or a religion? What does love have to do with death?

I also remember that on September 11, 2001, while I was a doctoral student south of Gailla, we saw an even more gigantic and spectacular disaster unfold before our eyes. I was working that evening in a warehouse that was unloading trucks from Italy, Poland, Spain, etc. We were listening to the radio, when suddenly the programs were interrupted and replaced by a special news bulletin. We were talking about the first tower of the World Trade Center in New York. A plane hijacked by terrorists had deliberately crashed into it, causing it to collapse. We were all ears when we learned that the other tower had just suffered the same fate with another plane that had plunged into it. Soon both were on the ground, in flames and dust. It didn't take long to hear that the Pentagon was also the victim of a plane crash. We were paralyzed, speechless and speechless! The slaughter of over three thousand souls that day was to dominate the news for at least the next three years.

Knowing Uncle Sam's Country, we knew it wouldn't go unpunished, no matter how long it took. So, George Bush kept his word when he attacked Afghanistan on October 7, 2001 to avenge America. Bingué and many other countries joined the coalition that aimed to dislodge the Taliban from power and get their hands on Osama Bin Laden, who had ordered the slaughter. Certainly, Ossama Bin Laden managed to evade and escape from his pursuers until the fateful day of May 2, 2011 when President Barack Obama accelerated his entry into Allah's paradise! I am sure he's having his fill with the beautiful seventy two heavenly brides that his God promised him fifteen hundred years ago!

Chapter 4

When social services in the West become an industry that produces young prostitutes, drug addicts, drug dealers and hardened criminals

A friend of mine, who lives in Neuchastel, had a daughter in a previous relationship. With the agreement of his wife, whom he met later, and who lived with him north of Bingué, he brought her to their home when she was about fourteen. In the following year, Ayesha, at fifteen, slept as she wanted. The Muslim father, unable to accept this debauchery with a good heart, corrected it by giving him belt shots. It took him badly. Ayesha went to report him to the police, saying that her father has been sexually abusing her since arriving in Bingué and that he is jealous to see her spending time with her boyfriend. She added that in his jealousy, he beat her violently with a belt.

The poor father, Kanté Siakoula, was arrested by the local police and detained. An investigation was carried out to verify the serious accusations brought against him by his daughter. After many negotiations, she had to withdraw her complaint and her father was released after several days of detention. He was on the verge of being tried and certainly condemned. Fortunately, there was little evidence that he had had incestuous sex with his underage daughter.

However, social services are riding on their high horse, as always, saying the man was an unworthy father, a paedophile, a sexual predator and that precautionary measures must be taken to protect his daughter by separating her from her family. . What was done. Ayesha was housed by social services in a place unknown to her parents.

After a year, her father, with a heavy heart, saw his daughter strolling through the streets of downtown Neuchastel with a stroller in which a new born baby was placed. She was barely sixteen and she had become a mother. She had fallen into prostitution and drugs. Seeing her father, she burst into tears remembering the worst moments of her life that he had suffered because of his slanderous denunciation that had landed him in irons. She told him all the misfortunes that had happened to her since she had left the family home to fall into the hands of the social services who left her to her own devices, with complete license to behave as she saw fit.

Together with other girls forcibly taken from their biological parents and who shared her refuge, they soon found themselves on the streets, partying until dawn, smoking first cigarettes, then cannabis. Several of them had tried heroin or cocaine. Several others had fatherless babies. She begged for her father's forgiveness so that he would take her back and reintegrate her into the family unit. But scalded cat is afraid of cold water. The father was really moved and sorry to hear his daughter's story, but he flatly refused to take her home again. He feared that she would once again accuse him of sexually abusing her, now that she had become a mother. Siakoula, a truck driver, did not want to risk losing his job in the event of an arrest that would tarnish his criminal record. Moreover, he did not want to risk being torn from the affection of his seven other children and his wife, Myriam.

This story also reminds me of that of Fistina, another Ebrounian compatriot from Bardamia who brought her eldest son to Bingué, born of a relationship prior to her marriage. The child was fifteen or sixteen years old and flew into a rage when his mother asked him to wash the dishes to help with the housework. He would doze off in class on the grounds that his mother made him a slave, demanding that he wash the dishes late at night and also in the early morning before going to class. Social services alerted, rushed to her home to snatch the boy. It has been more than ten years since he set foot with his mother, although he continues to live in the same city. He now looks like a madman: Rasta dreadlocks on his head, demonic tattoos on his body, with a ring in one ear. He is a drug addict who has failed his life and who lives like a tramp in this country which was supposed to give him a quality education for a future full of unexpected opportunities.

Exactly, Amah, the Ghanaian neighbour of Fistina made the same mistake by bringing her eldest son, Isaac, who had lived the first fifteen years of his life in his native Ghana. Enrolled in the public high school closest to Courbevoie, where the family home is located, he quickly befriended a gang of little high school thugs. Isaac was soon introduced to drug use and soon he would take a kitchen knife to extort money from his poor working mother to buy narcotics. He threatened to bleed his mother if she ever refused to give him money to buy his dose of drugs.

But when he turned sixteen, the worst was to happen. One day when he had finished taking his shower, under the influence of drugs, Isaac tied a towel around his loins to come and present himself in front of his mother, demanding that she undress so that he could make love to her. . He was threatening and wielding a knife, his eyes red with rage. The good lady must have told him that she is a woman and that she had not washed for several hours. For this, he would have to take a shower beforehand in order to be clean to have decent sexual relations. With that, the young man allowed him to go take a shower and come back to join him in the living room. He settled into the couch in the living room with a strong erection visible under his bath towel.

So, the mother slipped away and went into the shower with a hidden cell phone. She called the emergency services on 777 to tell them, in a whisper, of the danger that awaited her in the following minutes. Several police cars arrived at their home in less than five minutes and forced the door to find the young drug addict with his knife, comfortably installed in the armchair, waiting to rape his mother.

The brave mother took the opportunity to repatriate her narcotics-addicted son to his native Ghana, even if it meant getting drugs easily in this West African country. There are many examples like this, where African immigrants bring to Bingué their children born in Africa from a previous union, and who turn into monsters who try to swallow their parents. Several of them have denounced their parents to the police authorities or to the departmental social services for spurious reasons. These parents are systematically arrested, questioned, sometimes referred and judged. Several dismissals are pronounced and the parents recover their freedom with a lot of bitterness in the soul. Sometimes they were tried and then cleared, but a few were sentenced to firm prison terms.

However, the social cost of this bad way of doing things is heavy to bear because social services in the West have become an industry producing young prostitutes, drug addicts, drug dealers and hardened criminals who harm society as a whole. The dislocation of the family unit is the least of these costs while large-scale crime mourns the whole country with its procession of stabbings as we see every day in the metropolis of Londamou. It is especially young black people who pay the heaviest price for these settling of scores between rival gangs.

As the local proverb says: the crocodile that emerged from our urine bit us. It is our own children whom we fathered, whom we brought to the West because it was thought that they would study in excellent conditions and that they would have a much better chance of succeeding in life, who accuse us of all abuses: sexual abuse, beatings, slavery – if they are asked to wash the plates from which they themselves have eaten. Parents are arrested, sometimes judged, their careers in education or in social jobs, such as in retirement homes, are destroyed. The criminal record is dirty.

I can easily guess that the future of my daughters Alesha and Lydia is now in jeopardy. Already from the age of nine, Alesha wrote fiery love letters to the little boys in her class, spreading a story of her jealousy towards a rival who aimed at the same boy. These letters worried me to no end. I always wondered where this precocious sexuality came from. I called his mother, Maryline, who lived in Ebrounia, to take her to witness the actions of our daughter in common. I warned her that this little one would cause me serious problems and that she risked derailing my career as a secondary school teacher.

Once, in fact, in 2014, I remember that she had caused me a first alert which should have led me to repatriate her to Ebrounia to prevent the disaster of June 2017 from occurring. That day, I had asked her to get ready to go to school after she had missed a day due to a little illness. She obviously felt much better that day. But Alesha had squeezed her face, dragging her feet, deliberately, to delay her departure for classes. I couldn't wait to drive her there and ended up slapping her. Instinctively, she dodged the blow. Only the tip of my right index and middle finger had touched her left cheek. Not enough to whip a cat really. But she returned to class with a closed face, as if in mourning. When her teacher asked her why she looked so sad, she said that I had slapped her very hard on the face. The latter immediately seized the police and social services in accordance with child protection directives known as the Child Safeguarding and Protection Guide.

I had then gone to downtown Bardamia where we lived to buy some provisions for the house when Kyria, my wife, called me on my mobile phone to ask that I return home immediately because the police and the social services were waiting for me there. I was questioned that day on formal bail by the police and warned against slapping Alesha or any other child in the future. They threatened to take my children away from me if it happened again. As authorized punishments, I was told that I could confine the offending child to his room for a time, or beat him on the back of my hand with my simple fingers, in a light way, without leaving traces. I then called Maryline to inform her of my resolution to send Alesha back to her without delay, to prevent her from destroying my professional career because I had seven other children whose future I had to worry about. The latter had bent over backwards, begging my forgiveness because, she said, Alesha would have a much better chance of succeeding in Bingué than in Ebrounia. I let myself be touched by this speech that I should have ignored.

But today, June 8, 2017, I bitterly repent of not having followed my instinct in 2014. Because here I am in court here in Neuchastel to justify myself from the very serious accusations of Alesha. I find out in his charge sheet that I let my two daughters starve themselves for three long days and three nights in a row, her and her sister Lydia. However, they go to school and I pay their school canteen money every week at €25. I want to pay this amount out of my own pocket rather than sign up for free school meals because I was unemployed at the time. I therefore benefited from unemployment benefits which gave me the right to do so. But being a teacher myself, I knew from inside the house the segregation of children who were entitled to free meals. Their parents were known to be poor, school statistics made them children from whom nothing good should be expected. They were most often advised to follow alternative paths such as vocational training after a failed BEPC. This certificate of general secondary education was most often fatal to them in English, mathematics and science. However, they cannot progress to the general upper secondary cycle without having obtained a fairly good mention in each of these three essential disciplines. Statistics showed that these children ended up becoming criminals around the age of seventeen or eighteen. In class, their classmates whose parents worked laughed at them. In short, we could at least assume that Alesha and Lydia ate at least once a day on weekdays, in the school canteen. Their denominational school could testify to this. All that remained was to check what was reserved for them on the weekends.

At least on the day of my arrest, June 7, 2017, when the police came to my house, they saw that I had cooked to wait for the children who had to come home from school at half past three. There were potato fries on the menu, oven-roasted chicken thighs, and on the fridge there were ice creams, vanilla and chocolate Magnums, orange and pineapple juices, as well as soft drinks, coca-cola, Sprite and

Fanta cocktail. The officers went so far as to comb through the kitchen cupboards, top and bottom, to see what other uncooked groceries were there. They could see bags of rice, potatoes, boxes of chips of all tastes, biscuits, beef, mutton, frozen fish, frozen chicken thighs and many other things . Provisions for several weeks. Clearly, this was not a house where you didn't eat for days and nights in a row. And clearly the amount of meals cooked that day was not intended for one man, me, the father!

Alesha also claimed that I beat her regularly with belts, including two or three days before my arrest. The police therefore hoped to find fragments of Alesha's skin on my belts once they had been subjected to extensive forensic analysis. So the police had come up to my room, recovering my belts for investigation, and my passports, plus various documents, including the plane tickets I had already bought for the girls and me to go to Ebrounia July 21. They were to come and spend time with their respective mothers for the first time since arriving in Bingué. Alesha had not seen her mother for almost seven years. Admittedly, they saw each other on video every week because I called Maryline on Skype every week so that she could speak with her daughter. It was the same for Lydia who spoke to her mother, Pulchérie, on video every week.

A few weeks later, the same police were to write to me to inform me that absolutely no fragments of Alesha's skin had been found on my belts, nor Lydia's for that matter. No trace of their DNA was found on it either. There was only my DNA on my belts and no one else's. Also, the police invited me to pick up my belts and other personal effects taken on June 7. I just got my passport and plane tickets back but I gave up the belts I no longer wanted. All this for so little? The forensic harvest was very meager, as I told the court on June 8. I blamed myself absolutely nothing and nothing could incriminate me whatever the depth, length, breadth and thickness of the investigations carried out against me. I did not believe so well to say in front of the judge in charge of the case but the sequence of events proved me perfectly right. I was finally cleared by the Bingué police, although the scars of this scandalous affair remained indelible on my being.

When, on January 9, 2019, the General Council for Education cleared me of all suspicion again and rehabilitated me in my teaching profession, I breathed a big sigh of relief. I then obtained, on August 6, 2019, my new clean criminal record, which allowed me to walk again in a classroom in Bingué around September 10. That day, I spent at least four minutes praying in my inner being to give thanks to the Lord who had delivered me from the great waters and set me at sea. I bless his name for rehabilitating my humanity and restoring my professional career and reputation. I was no longer persona non grata. I was no longer an outcast, but a citizen who could walk tall among so many of his fellows. I could teach again and my white and black students would call me "Sir" again.

For too long I was no longer a gentleman, two and a quarter. But I had just risen from my ashes, like the Phoenix of mythology, and I was again wearing a well-tailored suit, with shirt and tie. I had become a teacher again. Hope was taking shape again over there, on the vast horizon, which opened before me.